Praise

Leslie Hill's *Dressed For Dancing* is a vivid journey to the heart of deep grief and back. From the first paragraph to the final lines, her compelling story and crisp, dynamic prose draw the reader into the quest for meaning after heartbreaking loss. When a skeptic joins a spiritual community, it could be sink or swim. Leslie plunges in boldly, and comes up sputtering for air. She describes her participation in the Findhorn Community with so much irreverent humour and deep gratitude that the reader is hard-pressed not to grab a carry-on bag and head for Scotland. *Dressed For Dancing* is a rollicking read that will move and delight and inspire, and show one woman's emergence from the shadow of sorrow into the spaciousness of a new life.

Marlene Schiwy, Ph.D, author of A Voice of Her Own:
Women and the Journal Writing Journey. *Fireside, 1996,
and* Simple Days: A Journal on What Really Matters.
Sorin Books, 2002

Dressed For Dancing drew me in from the first page and held me captivated throughout. Gracefully written, it has the excitement of a good novel but with the depth and insights that come from it being a true story of one woman's spiritual awakening and journey.

David Spangler, author of Apprenticed to Spirit.
Riverhead Books, 2011.

DRESSED FOR DANCING

My Sojourn in the Findhorn Foundation

LESLIE HILL

For Vida –
Alternative to bridge !
Leslie Althill

INCITE
P R E S S

VANCOUVER, CANADA

Incite Press
4101 Main Street, Box 74026
Vancouver, British Columbia
Canada, V5V 5C8
604-838-1406
incitepress@telus.net
www.lesliehill.ca

Sales. Request the book directly through your local book store, or order
on line, either through Amazon or www.lesliehill.ca

Editors: Wayde Compton, Betsy Warland. Copy Editor: Betsy Nuse.
Cover Photograph: Michael Julian Berz. Photograph of Author: Michael
Julian Berz. Cover Design: Frances Ishii. Text Design: Tamara
MacKenzie

Printed in the United States. First Edition.

Library and Archives Canada Cataloguing in Publication

Hill, Leslie, 1949 Nov. 30-
    Dressed for dancing: my sojourn in the Findhorn
Foundation/Leslie Hill

ISBN 978-0-9866127-5-6 (pbk.)

    1. Hill, Leslie, 1949 Nov. 30-. 2. Bereavement-Psychological
aspects. 3. Self-realization. 4. Findhorn Foundation. I. Title

BF575.G7H55 2012   155.9'37   C2012-905319-8

I dedicate this book to Paul James Sutton,
to The Findhorn Foundation,
and lastly, to Lilli Anathal Conradt
who persuaded me to write it.

Dressed for Dancing is my truth, as I see and remember it. Some names have been changed to avoid embarrassment. The identities of students and Findhorn Foundation guests are concealed to preserve confidentiality. To save the reader from confusion and exhaustion, a few of the people in the Findhorn Foundation speak for many.

Contents

CHAPTER 1
Good Days

I put our wedding photo on his bedside table. Not the one I would have chosen. I would have picked a more traditional one. This was Paul's choice, a casual shot of us, back to back, upper bodies only, our heads facing the photographer. He's smiling, I'm laughing. I didn't argue about the photo; this picture may not show off our clothes but our happiness blazes out of the frame. I was still delighted and grateful that he'd finally agreed to marry after eight years. I'd felt the connection the first week we spent together; for me it was obviously a permanent commitment. He saw the strong attraction, which, in his mind, didn't equal marriage.

But we did marry, in the end. Only six months ago. For a moment my sight blurred. If I'd been alone I would have cried, but I wasn't alone, even though Paul was asleep in the narrow hospital bed. The picture also doesn't show his thinness. The suit had fit him perfectly four weeks before the wedding but he'd lost weight by March 11.

All the stories in my childhood ended with the hero marrying the princess and living happily ever after. I was a thirty-nine year old professional, educated, logical, analytic, and a feminist, yet some part of me still believed I deserved a happy-ever-after ending. Putting the picture on the bedside table was an act of defiance.

I blinked until my vision cleared. I looked around the room, noted a new plant that had arrived since yesterday. A hibiscus with coral flowers and dark green leaves. Paul loved hibiscus. For him they symbolized the Caribbean, sun, heat and humidity, his respite through cold dark Canadian winters.

I'd tried to personalize the room to take the edge off the sterility but there's only so much you can do in a hospital. I'd taken down the crucifix – this was St. Joseph's - and put up a framed print of lilacs, another of Paul's favourites, brought in a tape recorder, his tea pot and tiny cup for the green tea he loved, and a single duvet in the same smoky blue as his eyes. It was September, and his windows looked south over Lake Ontario and west to the sunset. On windy days the large, single room got chilly. The staff had moved him here from a shared room on Labour Day weekend. It meant I could extend my visiting hours without disturbing anyone. I would have anyway; perhaps they realized or maybe it was the cookies I took regularly to the nursing station.

He stirred, waking, and opened his eyes. Reached for my hand as I leaned down to kiss him. He saw the wedding picture and smiled.

"Nice. I guess I fell asleep waiting for you. How was work?"

"Same old. Still pretty quiet this week. Lots of classes booked in next week for orientation."

"If you get too busy -"

"If I get too busy I'll take a day off work." I'd told my principal the week before school started that I would work from eight to four but not a moment longer. He'd nodded. Paul taught in another school in the same system. They knew. I didn't say much then, but the day the boss found me weeping in the library office when I should have been outside in the parking lot for our first fire alarm drill I had to admit that Paul's health wasn't improving, that I was sick with fear.

"Would you like me to make you some tea?"

"Love some. The hospital stuff is awful. I don't think they ever boil the water. And I hate those Styrofoam cups."

I made him green tea, in the little terra-cotta teapot he'd brought home from his four years in Japan. While it was steeping, he looked up at me, smiled a bit. "I've been thinking, we haven't made love since the end of July. Are you coping?"

I was torn between exasperation and amusement. "Coping? My dear idiot, you think sex is an issue? Don't you know what life is like for me when you're in here? I'm on automatic pilot outside this room. This time here, with you, every day, is the only time anything is real. I do what I need to to get through the day and live for the moments I'm with you."

His eyes widened and then he smiled. "Okay. I was just checking."

I poured tea into the small cup. He drank, closed his eyes for a moment. "That's delicious. Thanks."

When we first met, he'd been surprised by my readiness for lovemaking every time he turned to me. Decided I must be some hot woman. I didn't tell him otherwise, but the truth was that I never got over my own astonished delight at how much I loved him and how deeply he seemed to love me. I drank in every expression of it, from lovemaking to hand-holding to feeling his body next to mine as I drifted off to sleep at night. My earlier relationships had been poor, pallid things in comparison.

"Want a massage?"

He smiled and nodded. He loved being massaged. I poured some lotion into my hand, still warm from the tea pot, and pulled the duvet back from his feet and ankles. The duvet hid his wasted body, diminished now to skin stretched over bone, which made his swollen ankles look bizarre. I knew what the swelling meant. His circulation was failing. I began to rub cream into his right heel and instep with my thumbs, while my fingers held his foot steady. He closed his eyes. So did I. This was how we made love now.

We were quiet for a long time.

When I'd finished his second foot, ankle and calf he broke the silence.

"I don't think I could stand this without you. You're the most important person in the world. Your visits ... I'm grateful for every moment we're together. If I get out of here I'm going to make love to you every single day." He kissed the tips of my fingers, pulled me closer. My eyes clouded.

Later I went down to the cafeteria to get a sandwich and coffee and bring it upstairs to eat while he had his evening intravenous "meal" from a bag.

He showed me the new get well cards.

"The hibiscus is from Ralph. Nice, isn't it? Reminds me of the Virgin Islands. We'll go back, I hope. If we go in March, maybe you'll see another whale." He smiled at me. I actually loved the cold of winter, but the humpback whale, my first ever sighting a year ago, had completely reconciled me to a week down south every winter. Hibiscus bloomed everywhere there.

The sky grew gold and orange. Headlights swam through the dusk on Lakeshore Boulevard and the Gardiner Expressway.

We'd known for five years that this surgery was coming. Paul had had the first round in July 1984 to cut out a piece of small intestine so scarred from radiation after a childhood cancer of the kidney that food could no longer pass through it. He had agreed after increasingly frequent days of pain from food blockages and a dangerous loss of weight and energy. The doctor had warned us the scarring would build up again and more surgery would be necessary in five years or so.

Five years and one month.

On my way out after the visit, I went into the hospital chapel. As usual I was the only person in there. I didn't like God. I think it started with my Presbyterian upbringing. As a child I'd been afraid of the minister, an angry old Scot, who scowled down from the pulpit every Sunday and shouted his sermons. I focused on keeping a low profile. But I'd never doubted God's existence. I had prayed passionately when my mother was diagnosed with cancer at the age of fifty-two. Let her live, I'd pleaded. Her death four months later had killed my interest in God. I had stopped praying entirely.

But after eleven years of avoiding both God and church, I'd been coming here daily, ever since the assistant surgeon had spoken to me in the hall, three days after Paul's surgery. He was asleep and I was leaving. She had spoken in a brisk matter-of-fact voice.

"We began the operation on schedule, but when we reached the site of the scarred intestine we found a number of small growths that are clearly malignant. We then had to decide whether or not to proceed as planned, to remove the scarred section of intestine or to cancel the surgery and just close him up. That discussion is why the operation took longer than we had anticipated. Eventually we agreed that his quality of life would be better with the surgery so we went ahead." She waited for me to respond.

It took me a moment. I had to clear my throat, find my voice. I could hear a quaver as I spoke. "I don't understand. Why didn't you remove the growths? You were right there."

"There were far too many of them. They are scattered like pepper all through his abdominal area."

"Oh. But – what can you do then? He can't have more radiation."

"No. But we might try chemo, when he has recovered. If there is pain." She waited but I couldn't speak. My mind was a blank. I kept hearing her words over and over. *Clearly malignant. Quality of life. Scattered like pepper.*

I felt my way out of the hospital that day.

The chapel was silent, with peach coloured walls and subtle lighting that suggested windows even though there were none. When I closed my eyes, light seemed to shine more brightly than it did when my eyes were open. It was very peaceful.

I might not think much of God, but Paul was an atheist. He wouldn't see any of the hospital clergy. I was the only one who did believe who visited him daily. So I tried God again. But there was no point praying for Paul to live, since it hadn't worked for my mother.

I waited until I figured God had noticed me, to make my plea.

"Let me channel divine love to him. Let my love be as pure and as holy as possible, since he won't accept You in any other way. Let me bring him as much comfort and strength as You might. Help me."

I had no idea what God would make of such a prayer from someone who disliked Him but I didn't care. Paul had been more relaxed and I'd been less panicky since my first chapel visit. Nothing else mattered.

The silence deepened and the peach coloured light steadied me. I sat, letting the peace of the place quiet my fears.

Paul's health had been problematic as long as I'd known him. Not a completely bad thing. It meant he made the most of the good days. He was usually so positive, so upbeat that I was surprised the day I heard him criticize another teacher for looking forward to the summer holidays.

"The fool is pissing his life away," he'd said impatiently. "Every moment counts. I can't understand someone getting bored or upset over nothing at all."

That was when I understood it wasn't a coincidence that our relationship was so good. Paul didn't waste time. He didn't bicker, quarrel, fall into bad moods. When we argued, it was about something important. Without realizing it, I'd followed the pattern he set. For eight years life had been marvellous, even in the shadow of his ill health.

But our good days were running out.

CHAPTER 2
Ending

I was asleep on my side of the bed when the phone rang. I peered at the clock. 2 a.m. It was Paul's line so I stumbled out to his study to answer, too groggy to wonder who could be calling.

"Leslie Hill?"

"Yes."

"I'm Dr. Morgan, the on-call doctor tonight at St. Joseph's Hospital. I'm sorry to have to tell you that your husband has passed away."

Silence.

I shook my head. This was a mistake.

"No, that can't be true. He wasn't much worse than usual when I saw him tonight. At least … I mean … he can't really be …"

"I'm afraid it is true. Why don't you come to the hospital?"

"Now?"

"Yes."

So I dressed and drove obediently through the empty streets to St. Joseph's. Drove perfectly. I stopped for red lights, even for amber warning lights. Somewhere inside me pressure was building, like a howl, but I sat at the wheel rigidly controlled and noticed what an easy drive it was at 2:30 a.m. How silent but pleasant the streets were. First time in a month I'd been able to park near the entrance. I took meticulous care to line the car up exactly with the car in front and the car behind. Then I walked composedly in through the Emergency entrance.

I took the elevator up to the familiar floor and turned my face away from the door to the chapel. A doctor was waiting at the nursing station. He looked young and tired.

"Mrs. Sutton?"

I opened my mouth to correct him but ended up nodding. He didn't touch me. His dark eyes held an expression I couldn't read.

"I'm Dr. Morgan. I'm sorry for your loss. Your husband died of a pulmonary embolism, a blood clot in the lungs." He walked toward Paul's room so I followed. He talked on but I no longer heard him. A blood clot. Unable to breathe, must have panicked, reached out, clutched, frantic for air, found nothing. I hadn't been there. Maybe no one had.

At the door the doctor paused. "Can you do that?"

"What?"

"Can you pack up his clothing and personal items and take them with you?"

"Now?"

"Yes."

"All right."

He opened the door.

Paul lay straight and quiet on the bed. The sheets and hospital blanket looked unnaturally crisp and smooth, tucked neatly under his arms. Whatever struggle or violence had occurred here had been erased. The blue duvet lay folded on a chair. The IV stand, the bags and tubes and medical paraphernalia were gone. The perfection of the order and tidiness was unreal. The doctor vanished. The silence was absolute. It could have been a stage set, except that in the centre was Paul, so familiar, so still.

I sat down in the chair by the bed and took his hand. It was neither warm nor cold; room temperature. After a few moments my voice emerged, wavering and weak, growing stronger as the words came.

"Oh Paul, I had no idea this was so close. I wish I'd said more this evening when I said goodbye. I wish …" I stopped. Started again. "We did well, as well as we could have, through this summer, this month. I know how hard you tried to live. I'm … so grateful for everything we've done together, the laughter, the adventures, the travelling, all of it. Your love. Thank you for ... marrying me."

I heard footsteps in the corridor. They slowed, then retreated. I looked at Paul's face, thin and hollowed, the fine fair hair, the straight nose, the beautifully curved mouth, the colourless skin. "I'll be all right. Don't worry."

I kissed him. On his hand, and his cheek. Then gathered the possessions, the Scrabble game we didn't use, the Japanese teapot and cup, the duvet, the little tape recorder, the poster of lilacs. Our wedding picture. His clothes and toiletry bag. The flowering hibiscus in its container. I stacked them in a wheelchair someone had left in the hallway. Pushed the loaded wheelchair down the hall and out to the car in a trance. Put the possessions in the car. Drove home slowly.

I carried in the plant but left the rest. In the kitchen I put the kettle on without thinking, and made a cup of tea. Took it upstairs to Paul's study and sat down at the desk. Nearly 4 a.m. I would wait until dawn to call his mother and my father, who would tell me what to do next.

CHAPTER 3

Night Watch

I turned on the old-fashioned brass desk lamp, sat in the burgundy desk chair, my hands wrapped around the mug of tea, and looked around Paul's study.

"I'm a widow," I said aloud, but the words had no meaning.

This room was completely Paul's. I'd contributed nothing. He'd chosen the colours, grey walls and burgundy accents. He'd chosen to have an alcove instead of a cupboard with an antique washstand there to hold his files. Above it hung old family photos in ornate, dark wood frames. A huge desk, a rocking chair, a small chest in the bay window. Two sectional oak bookshelves held his books on house renovations, sailing, computers, small businesses, tax information, school yearbooks and the building plans for this house. No blinds or curtains on the east-facing bay window. He liked maximum light. Photos he'd taken of the house and the sailboat, framed with burgundy matts, on the wall near the desk. The desk calendar beside the telephone said Wednesday September 27th. I looked at the telephone. His business line. It would have his voice message. I could hear him speak. If I did that ...

I wondered if I would go mad.

He always paid attention to decor. I remembered the first time I'd been to his apartment. He had taken me out to dinner. When he brought me back his place felt cool and fresh. He opened the blinds so I could see the view, south over the Humber River. The water shone silver in the evening light until it curved into the shadow of trees. I sat on the floor with my back against a deep blue love seat and waited for him to pull me into his arms.

We made love for the first time on the floor of his living room, the wool carpet rasping against my naked body. Later we moved into his bed. I felt the foam mattress mould itself around me and the cool sheets become warm.

"Comfortable?" he murmured.

"Very."

"Tired?"

"No."

He laughed. "Come here, then."

His body was slight and muscular. His lovemaking was like coming home.

I woke once from sleep in the night to find him coming back to bed with two glasses of water. He offered me one, drank half of his and then put his fingers in the rest and trailed them over and around my naked breasts until heat rose up to scorch my skin and I pulled him on top of me, knocking over my glass.

He made love to me with immense care, as if every moment counted and there were a finite number of moments. I lay bathed in a sea of sensuality; for me time had ceased.

In the morning he made me tea and eggs with sharp cheddar cheese and red pepper on toast. The kitchen was a bright spring green. A white wooden lattice separated the eating and cooking areas. It was clean, uncluttered, original. I looked around, impressed with the room, breakfast, him.

It was impossible to believe he was dead. For eight years and three months he had been the rock, the foundation, the centre of my existence. Who was I now?

CHAPTER 4

Planning

The busyness of death took over that day. I didn't have to figure out who I was. I didn't have to do anything but accept direction. My family, father, stepmother, sister, brother and sister-in-law arrived to organize and support and set up. I simply did what I was told. In between instructions, I stalled, with no idea what to do next.

My step-mother and sister-in-law cleaned and bought groceries. I'd let everything go since Paul had gone into hospital, four and a half weeks ago. *How could he have gone in for routine surgery and died four and a half weeks later? At forty-nine?* My brother and father made the necessary phone calls. My sister and father took me to the funeral home, picked up forms and prodded me into decisions around casket, funeral home visits and the memorial service. I knew Paul had wanted to be cremated.

The minister, Deborah, arrived mid-afternoon. I didn't know her well. She hadn't even been my first choice, just the one who was available. She had never met Paul. She was perhaps ten years younger than me, with brown eyes and hair and beautiful skin. She sat down, leaned forward and radiated such warmth and sympathy that I knew she would understand how extraordinary he was.

"Tell me about Paul," she said.

I felt as if she had opened a door. I stepped through and began to talk.

"We've been together eight years and a few months. We met when we took our students to a five day residential program on leadership skills and anti-racism. We led one of the groups together." I paused for a moment. Deborah listened with her whole attention, her eyes fixed on my face.

"I fell in love with him that week. From the start we balanced each other. I've always kept a distance with students. When I got there and realized I had to speak and listen from the heart, I was petrified. But Paul was relaxed and funny. He didn't talk a lot but he made it easier for all of us. The kids were so brave, talking about their experiences, that I found it hard to stay – detached. I'm usually very – controlled but ... well. In my family we don't ... don't cry or get angry, ever. So this ... it was a challenging week. On the third night, Paul gave me feedback about my strengths. It was a communications exercise with the group and he said ..." I drew breath. I could see him, so clearly. "'I know you really want us all to get a lot out of this week. I love how much you care.' I was blown away. No one ever – I always tried to fit a role, to be competent, to be what other people expected. He saw past all that and loved what he saw. I didn't have to do anything. He just – loved me. I knew, right then."

I passed a hand across my eyes. "No one has ever loved me so simply. No expectations. It was a miracle. Like taking off a straitjacket I'd worn my whole life, one I didn't even know was there.

"He spent four years in Japan teaching with his first wife. You'll meet her at the funeral. She had left him, but they stayed good friends. He never held grudges against anyone. Not her, or difficult colleagues or tough students ... I admire him for it. I don't forgive people so easily. On our first date he took me to a Japanese restaurant and spoke Japanese to the chef. I was dazzled. I went to bed with him that night." I smiled. "We've celebrated special events with Japanese food ever since.

"He has a wonderful sense of humour. We laugh, so much." I stopped, remembering our lovemaking, riddled with laughter, teasing, the touch of his hands in the darkness, the strength of his arms, the warmth of his body.

"He can be stubborn. I wanted to marry him right away but he wouldn't, too damaged by the end of his first marriage. I don't think he trusted me to stay through the difficult times because she hadn't. But I did. I never thought of anything else. And last October he finally proposed to me. We've been a couple for eight years, lived together since his first round of surgery five years ago, but we've only been married for six months. It was a miracle. I never thought I'd marry. I'm thirty-nine. Old for a first marriage, but -" Young to be widowed. For a moment, I couldn't speak. Married and widowed at thirty-nine. I felt a rushing in my ears. Waited until it cleared. Deborah waited too, completely still.

"He never expected me to be anything other than what I was. Never tried to dominate me and didn't let me tell him what to do. Sometimes I tried to." I smiled. "He would listen but make up his own mind. So did I. We are equals. I've never had that in a relationship before. This is the first time I've ever felt safe enough to be equal.

"He was so excited when he learned that I like sailing. He'd always wanted to sail. He bought an Alberg 30, and we spent summers in Georgian Bay ..."

I remembered his delight as he held the tiller, keeping the boat close to the wind, so it heeled over and we laughed aloud and planted our feet so we wouldn't slide. Remembered sitting in the twilight, watching beaver swim in the bay, listening to loons calling. The beauty would always take my breath away, as if I were seeing it for the first time. Swimming ourselves, sometimes at midnight, when it was really hot. Then sliding into bed together, skin like cool silk.

"He would have made a good father, but we couldn't have children. Sometimes I wondered if I would miss them but I never have. He's been enough."

It had been a month after we'd first made love before Paul told me that he was sterile, that he'd had cancer on one kidney as an infant and that the radiation after the surgery had killed all possibility of children. I was thirty-one. I hadn't believed I would ever love anyone enough to marry, so children hadn't figured much in my plans. Besides, we were high school teachers and our lives were filled with kids. So I hadn't hesitated. I didn't regret my decision.

But I had thought he would live – we would live together - for years.

"He never had any use for the church." I hesitated but Deborah's sympathetic expression didn't change. "He would never say why, but he's a good man. We got married at the Caledon Inn, in the tiny pub. He owns - owned the place. It sounds odd but it was lovely, in front of the fire, twenty family members there to witness. The sun shone through the window as we were signing the form. Like a blessing."

The morning of our wedding I'd felt more calm, centred and serene than I've ever been.

"We've just finished a year off work together. We've travelled, camped, sailed, spent all our time together. Got married. He's adventurous, persuades me to try a lot of different things. He's so alive. It's been ... such a wonderful year until the last couple of months. I guess we've been lucky, really."

I thought of our road trip across the States, whale watching in the Bay of Fundy, his proposal, our wedding in March. Trips to Barbados and to Britain. Lovemaking. Our laughter. My happiness. His slow fade as fatigue and illness began to erode his energy. Remembered he was dead.

"He was so sexy," I whispered. I couldn't say any more. There was a long, unbroken silence.

Finally Deborah pulled a notebook and pen from her purse.

"Tell me the names of family members I'll meet at the funeral." She wrote the names down carefully. "Do you know what scripture you'd like read?"

"The one from Corinthians about love. You know, 'if I speak with the tongues of men and angels and have not love ...'"

She hesitated. "That's - usually chosen for weddings."

"I can't help that. That's how he loved. That's how he treated everyone, not just me. That's what I want heard and remembered."

She smiled. "That's what we'll use then."

CHAPTER 5
Interim

E veryone went home eventually. I was alone. Twenty-four hours ago Paul had been alive. Some time later I went to bed. I don't know if I slept or when I woke.

The next morning I made tea and toast. Sat at the dining room table in a pool of sunshine. The house was silent. I had a pen and piece of paper beside me. My sister had told me to make To Do lists, one for the next week, one for the following three weeks, one for the next three months. Very practical. I wrote down the headings and sat looking at the paper. Nothing occurred to me.

My best friend, my husband, is dead and I'm staring at a To Do list. Bizarre. I don't feel anything. I must be in shock. Maybe that's good. I leaned back, felt the sun warm my shoulders. *I wonder what will happen when it wears off. I wonder if I'm going to get through this. Maybe I won't. Maybe I'll commit suicide.*

"Oh no you won't." The voice, intense and emphatic, came out of nowhere. I glanced around. No one outside the window, no one in the house. I even looked down at my own abdomen. But I hadn't spoken.

It didn't make sense.

Nothing made sense.

After a while, I turned back to my list.

CHAPTER 6
Funeral

The funeral home visits and my family kept me upright. I had to stand and greet people, not think, not feel. I knew this from my mother's funeral. Emotion was private. It would come later, when I was alone. I put a picture of Paul from our wedding on top of the closed casket.

Family, friends, colleagues came and went. Sometimes I almost forgot why I was there as I chatted to people. His ex-wife was there throughout. I stood by the coffin, she near the door. Neither of us cried. When the Italian teacher from Paul's school burst into noisy sobs, I handed her a tissue. She looked at me as if I were an alien.

My face felt very warm. When I looked at myself in the Funeral Home mirror, my cheeks were scarlet. I'd automatically applied blush before leaving home but this was more than blush. I patted cold water on my face, but my colour remained hectic.

One of my cousins said how unfair it was, that I'd been widowed before the honeymoon was over. I stared. This made no sense. We'd had eight years of honeymoon. If I'd had the whole eight years over again, knowing where we'd end, I wouldn't do anything differently. There was nothing to regret. I straightened, stood taller.

I survived three funeral home visits and the memorial service.

After the service the Ladies Aid put out coffee, tea and cake. I greeted more people. Eventually my father drove me back to his apartment on Old Mill Road, where my stepmother had put out a cold lunch for family. I nodded and smiled, accepted a bouquet of red roses from my favourite aunt, managed as long as I could.

Then, abruptly, I felt exhausted and knew I had to be alone. I left, and walked up the Humber River to our home, carrying my roses. It was the last day in September, a sunny Saturday afternoon. There were wedding parties everywhere, at the Old Mill Inn, in the park, lining up for pictures. I looked at them, bright with colour, fluttering with laughter and excitement, fragile as butterflies. Make it count, I whispered to them. Make every moment count.

CHAPTER 7
Psychic Reading

I said I'd return to school after Thanksgiving Weekend. No one argued.
I reminded myself that I came from a long line of survivors on both sides. My parents believed in work, stiff upper lips, stoicism. You didn't weep and wail, you didn't give in, you Went On With Things. I had no idea how I'd live through this, but I didn't question it. Paul had survived cancer as an infant, the end of a marriage, years of ill health and never complained. He was critical of people who gave up. I was only thirty-nine, a professional teacher, intelligent, analytic, practical and pragmatic. I'd be fine. Eventually.

At home I began mechanically to tackle the To Do list. I deleted his message from the tape without listening to it, because I knew that if I heard him speak I'd never be able to erase his voice. While Paul had been in the hospital I'd bought new sheets and a duvet cover to welcome him home. I put these on the bed immediately without letting myself contrast my hopeful purchase with the bleak present. I emptied clothes from his drawers, put some aside for friends but gathered most for a refugee family sponsored by the church. I tackled paperwork an hour or so at a time, grateful that he'd been so organized and orderly. I packed up items from Japan to give to his ex-wife, family pictures for his sister and his father's pocket watch for his oldest nephew. I made an appointment with the lawyer who was the executor of his will. At first I worked quickly. Then I wondered what it would be like when I finished, and slowed down abruptly.

I knew enough not to drink.

On Monday, two days after the funeral, I took the leftover cans of the diet supplement prescribed back to the doctor's office. I dumped the box on the receptionist's desk and left quickly. I hadn't really cried since Paul had died and didn't want to start weeping in public.

Outside at the Jane and Bloor Street intersection, I blinked rapidly to beat back the tears. When the blurring cleared, I saw a battered sandwich sign across the street. *Psychic Readings.* I knew this corner well but I'd never seen the sign before. I crossed the road, opened the door, climbed the stairs.

A woman about my age, in jeans and a green sweatshirt, looked over the railing.

"You want a reading? Thirty bucks. Come in here." She pointed to a sagging armchair in a cluttered living room, then sat down across from me with a coffee table between us. I handed her the money.

"I don't need to know anything about the past or the present. Just the future please."

"I tell you what I see, I don't do time lines." She shuffled a grubby looking deck of cards and handed it to me to cut. "Use your left hand."

She turned the first card over without a comment. Put down the second.

"Looks like you've been having a rough time lately."

When she turned over the third, she shot a glance at me. I stared fixedly at the cards, which meant nothing to me and were blurring anyway.

"You've ended a relationship lately, lost someone important to you." There was a faint question in her words.

"My husband. He died. Yes."

"When?"

"Wednesday."

"Last Wednesday?"

I nodded. She put down the deck of cards. "But – why are you coming to see me?"

"Because you can't say anything bad. Whatever you see can't be worse than now. I thought, if you looked forward, you'd see something better, something that would ... I don't know, help me move on."

It seemed perfectly logical to me, but she stared in disbelief. Finally she shook her head, picked up the cards again and started laying them out and talking fast.

"You're going to have a hard time for quite a while. Work is difficult. I see minor health problems that you might have to deal with long term. Not everyone around you is as supportive as they seem. Someone is going to demand a lot of you that you can't give and that person will be very angry with you. You'll be doing some travelling but it won't make much difference to the way you feel for a few years. Christ. Look, give me your right hand."

She had changed tactics so quickly that it took me a moment, but I flattened my hand in hers. She stared grimly at the lines in my palm and then relaxed.

"Okay, here's some good news. You're going to live to be over ninety."

I burst into tears.

CHAPTER 8

Isolation

I cried quite a bit after that visit to the psychic, in fits and starts. I was alone so it didn't upset anyone. The house that Paul and I had designed together felt like a tomb. We'd spent the whole year off work in a world of our own, except for our wedding, and now I was completely alone.

I returned to school after Thanksgiving weekend. Work had held me together through the months when my mother was dying and afterward. It would hold me together now. Hard work was a good antidote to grief. Hard work and a routine to connect me to a life without Paul.

Tuesday morning at 7:50 I unlocked the door to the library and entered. For a moment I stood and looked around. Pale light shone in the north- and west-facing windows. The chairs and tables, computer catalogues, bookshelves, book trucks, green plants were exactly as I expected but somehow unfamiliar. I fumbled for the light switch, unlocked the workroom door, put my purse in the cupboard. Remembered I had to turn on the banks of computers and looked around for the power switches. Nothing had changed. But everything seemed strange.

When Jim, the library technician, came in ten minutes later, I was sitting at my desk in the middle of the library still wearing my jacket.

"Good morning. I'm glad you're back," he said. "Are you all right?"

"Yes." But I didn't move. He put his coat away, turned on his computer. I could feel him watching me so I stood up. It took me a while to remember to check the reservations book to see what was scheduled to happen today. Four classes had signed in to use the library, but I wasn't required to teach them.

"There are groups waiting to book you but we agreed to give you a day or so."

I nodded. "Thanks. That's – good."

By the end of the day I was white with fatigue. The days after that were the same. I felt disconnected from the work, the staff and the students. Nothing was automatic.

Everything I did felt as if I were walking through water. Even people's voices were distorted, as if I were behind some kind of invisible barrier. Meaning lagged well behind sound. When I climbed into my car in the parking lot on the first Friday after my return, I was so exhausted I could barely put my key into the ignition. I wondered if I had the strength to drive home. I got there but when I stepped inside, the house was empty. Paul wasn't there. I realized I'd been expecting him. I crumpled up on the couch and cried.

Somehow I kept going, one foot in front of the other, and an automatic pilot did kick in. Much of the time I was numb. I welcomed that numbness, it was easier. But sometimes tears leaked anyway, even without a trigger. At home it didn't matter. At work I could usually withdraw into my office until the tears had passed. Once on the street I turned into an alley, sobbing, crouched down, my head against a brick wall like a homeless person.

I knew I wasn't okay but I struggled on. I didn't know what else to do. Somehow I survived the worst moments: a late wedding gift of six champagne glasses; the evening the minister came over for a visit and I thought about God, taking away my husband; my fortieth birthday, when my father and his wife arrived at the library with balloons marked Happy 40th although I'd begged them to ignore it; Christmas alone; the life insurance cheque arriving in the mail, the biggest amount of money I'd ever seen, and I looked at it, an exchange for my husband, and began to shake with rage. I had to slam it shut in a drawer to keep myself from ripping it into pieces.

But moments of such strong feeling were rare. I honestly believed that if I waited long enough, I'd wake up some day and be happy, the way I was before I'd met Paul. My father had married another woman eight months after my mother's death. My grandfather had done the same. My brother fell in love with someone four months after his wife had left him for someone else. My family endured; survived; went on. I assumed I would too.

But the process wasn't working like that. This time work was not an antidote to grief. It meant almost nothing to me, a job that I had once loved. I still worked hard but working exhausted me.

When the friends and family who were not avoiding me asked me how I was, I could not pretend. My lifetime pattern of polite, restrained, considerate behaviour vanished. I told them I felt like shit and tried not to say I wished I were dead. Increasingly though, dead looked good.

My family didn't know what to make of me. They expected me to be cheerful at best, stoic at worst. Not lost.

My father and his wife invited me over to dinner once a week and sent me home with leftovers in a Tupperware container. My sister came over one night after work carrying a black plastic box.

"Paul's ashes," she said. "I didn't think you should have to pick them up yourself."

"Thank you." For such a small box it was surprisingly heavy. I stood, holding it awkwardly, unsure what to do with it.

"Why not just put it on the bookshelf until you know what you want to do," she said.

"Right." I cast around for a change of topic. "I've just been shopping. Do you want to see what I've bought? By the way I'm worried about Dad. He looks older."

She followed me into the bedroom where the new suit, shirt, pants and sweater were lying on the bed. "He's worried about you, that's why he looks older."

"Why? I'm managing."

"Are you? Did you think about colour when you bought these?"

"What do you mean?" I looked down at the bed. I hadn't bought anything other than my wedding dress for a year, and the purchases were overdue.

"Colour. Red, blue, green, remember? The brightest thing you've got here is white."

It was true. The suit was gray, the pants and sweater black.

"Black is in, that's all."

"Black is always in. That doesn't mean you have to wear it non-stop."

"I'm doing the best I can, okay?"

"I know. That's why Dad is worried."

They were all trying so hard to help me. Everyone said the first year was the hardest. I just had to get through that.

I'd heard that newly widowed women were seen as easy prey by married men, but no one ever made a pass at me. I wondered why. I certainly felt as if I'd been without sex for a long time. I didn't want a relationship, but a night of sex might make me feel alive for a little while.

Kathleen, one of my teaching friends, suggested I take up downhill skiing. I hadn't skied since I'd been in my twenties but supposed skiing would fill the empty weekends. With her help I bought equipment, ski clothes and a season's ski pass at Blue Mountain. I rented a room in her chalet for the winter. On New Year's Day a friend of hers came up to join us, a man I'd met several times over the years. He showed up at the central lift at Blue Mountain and hugged me. I recoiled so violently I nearly fell.

"For Chrissake, it's only a New Year hug," he said.

"Sorry, I ... you just took me by surprise."

"Sure." He skied off to another lift. I was baffled. I wanted contact. How had my body disconnected so completely from my mind?

One night, about five months after Paul's death, I decided to make a stir-fry for dinner, a step up from the boiled egg or pasta I had most nights. I lined up onion, garlic, zucchini, carrots, broccoli. As I brought the knife down on the onion I sliced my thumb open. Surprised, I ran the cut under cold water and pressed a paper towel on it until the bleeding stopped. Five minutes later, chopping a carrot, I cut the same thumb, different place, just as deeply. This time I went into the bathroom, still carrying the knife. I put it on the edge of the sink, wadded toilet paper around the thumb and held my hand above my head to stop the bleeding. While I waited, I stared at myself in the mirror. Left hand and white wadded thumb in the air, white face, dark circles under my eyes, skinny. I looked like the walking dead.

The knife lay there, a shred of carrot still on the blade. I rinsed it and held it to my neck. It would be easy, wouldn't it, to press the knife into my throat, slice through an artery, slump over the toilet so the blood flowed into the bowl? Let go of these futile attempts to keep going. Release. Relax. I watched myself in the mirror. The knife blade glittered.

The knife had been a wedding present.

I couldn't do it. Not without at least trying to get help. They'd never understand, never forgive me or themselves. I left the knife on the edge of the bathroom sink, abandoned the dinner and sat down in the rocking chair that had been my mother's. Wept.

CHAPTER 9

Present and Past

Two days later I sat across a desk from Bill, a therapist, whose company had a contract with my Board of Education. Three free sessions on any concern, confidentiality assured. I didn't actually give a shit about confidentiality. If the Board of Education couldn't understand grief, I didn't want to work for them.

I can see now that a woman therapist would have been better. The only man I wanted to see then was Paul. Bill seemed faded, nondescript. He had pale hair, washed-out blue eyes, pallid skin. I didn't want to look at him. Plus I hated being vulnerable in front of a man. But he was free and I needed help.

"Why are you here?" His voice was stronger than I expected.

I opened my mouth to say I'd always been a happy person and I wanted that back. Without warning I was assaulted by memories of being lonely and isolated as a child, spending Saturdays reading, standing alone in a school yard, being left out of giggling discussions about boys. For a moment I felt dizzy and disoriented. Did I know anything about myself?

"I ... I was widowed in September and I'm not ... I can't ... I don't know how to ... get past it. Nothing seems to help. I don't know why," I whispered at last.

"You're saying you feel derailed by the grieving process?"

"I guess."

"Let's talk about that."

I was terrified.

It took me years to understand why I found therapy so difficult at first. Now I know that I was conditioned to believe that tears, anger and vulnerability indicated weakness. Weakness was bad; self-control was good. My parents were calm, pleasant people who discussed things rationally and led us to believe that nothing else was appropriate. I loved and admired them. When I was overwhelmed by unhappiness or anger, my mother said I must be tired and sent me to my room. It was crystal clear that strong feeling made other people uncomfortable, and that was unacceptable. If I couldn't squash the feelings, I had to be alone until they were under control. I remember being tired a lot. Sometimes it was hard to tell which came first, tiredness or emotion.

So when I was unable to control a "negative" emotion, I became both tired and frightened. After a couple of sessions with Bill, I acknowledged that I'd survived this long, seven months, so I wasn't likely to commit suicide, but I could easily imagine waking up some morning and deciding to stay in bed. Forever. I was afraid that examining "the grieving process" would unleash so much grief I'd sink under it for good. But I was sinking anyway, so I agreed.

I talked mostly about Paul in these sessions, my life with and without him. I would begin crying on the subway, on route to Bill's office. I'd cry all through the session and all the way home. Every night I'd write in my journal and cry some more. The tears might have dried up by the end of the week, but my next appointment would begin the cycle all over again.

To my dismay, my grief wasn't just about Paul. Old griefs emerged from everywhere. My ability to hold back the past had somehow disappeared, as if the therapy sessions had unlocked a floodgate. I didn't mention this to Bill; I felt neurotic enough already. Instead I tried to make a list of griefs one night as I sat at the computer. If I could identify them, maybe I could box them up again.

A family move to Toronto when I was sixteen. I remembered the utter misery of my Grade 12 year, when no one at my new school even noticed I was there.

Even as I typed the first item on my list, the past came alive, grief spilling everywhere, right here, right now.

Robin, the dog, put down by my parents when he was ten. I'd seen him a couple of weeks earlier, hadn't even known he was ill. They told me by phone two days after his death. I could feel his silky, silver topknot in my fingers as I typed, see his almond shaped brown eyes, his wagging tuft of a tail. Tears poured down my face and the print on the computer screen dissolved.

My mother's death in April, 1978.

My father, grey faced and remote. My brother, sister and I struggling to be calm and tearless because that's what my father wanted. He didn't have to say it; we all knew. Even with her Scottish Presbyterian background, my mother wasn't quite as skilled at keeping her feelings hidden as my father, but she tried hard. Until her death, I'd worshipped my father. But when she was gone, I saw for the first time that she, not he, was the heart of the family. Guilt piled on grief. Why hadn't I seen it when she was alive?

I tried so hard all those years to keep my grief to myself, hid in my room whenever I couldn't hold back the tears, until the fall of 1978.

My father's remarriage.

When Mum was diagnosed with a brain tumour and hospitalized, I moved home to look after my father. My sister, immersed in her second year of law school, spent all her time in the library. I cooked, cleaned and the rest of it every night. After Mum died, I stayed on, unable to see my father struggle without help. Maybe his struggle was largely in my mind. In September he asked a neighbour to set him up with someone. After four or five dates with a widow, Dad brought a bottle of wine home for Friday night dinner. I was surprised but delighted. He usually drank Scotch, but my sister and I preferred wine. Marg was in for once, and I was congratulating myself on the dinner when Dad asked how we'd liked Joan, whom he'd introduced to us two days earlier.

"Very nice," I said, wondering if I could manage a turkey at Thanksgiving.

"She seems pleasant," said my sister.

"Well, I wasn't cut out to be a single man. I've asked Joan to marry me, and she's said yes."

There was a ringing silence. I looked at my father, then at my sister, then at the glass of wine my father had poured me.

"Fast work," said my sister, smiling.

I was the oldest. I knew what my mother would have expected me to do. I tried.

"Congratulations," I said, raising my glass, "on your .... your ..."

I couldn't do it. A river of tears poured down my face. My sister looked away. My father looked politely bemused.

"I thought you said you like her," he said.

"I did. I do. It's just ... I'm still mourning Mum, every day, and you ... you ... I feel like you're burying her all over again, only deeper." I scrubbed the tears off my face with a napkin, lifted the wine glass again as fresh tears streamed down, and said steadily, "Congratulations on your marriage plans."

The toast fell flat. At least my sister wasn't crying. An hour later Dad went out to see his fiancée and Marg to see her law school friends. I cleaned the kitchen and went to my room. By the time I came out, I was back in control.

I stayed that way for eleven years.

But now ...

So much for boxing up old griefs. I put my head in my hands and cried until I was drained.

CHAPTER 10
Grief Work

I wanted my self-control back. I wanted to know I would not cry outside of my home, or Bill's office. But after a few months of therapy, the best I could say was that I was less afraid of exploding in public. Some of the pressure had been released.

But my negativity was increasing. I hated my emotions, the disruptiveness of them. I disliked my brothers-in-law, who were so much less than Paul and who were alive. I refused dinner invitations to couples' places because I resented the husbands. I disliked Bill, the weekly witness to my emotional weakness. I resented my need for therapy, which my father called "navel gazing." He thought I should feel sad for a couple of months and then marry again, just as he had.

On my first wedding anniversary, I taught all day, prepped for two hours and then exhausted myself at the local gym. That meant I could sleep. But sleep was not a refuge. I dreamed about being in a rowboat alone without oars on a dark, endless sea. Sometimes I dreamed about Paul, dreams so vivid that when I woke I couldn't believe he was dead. Both asleep and awake I'd find myself listening for his footstep, coming to help me sort out problems I couldn't face.

Migraine headaches began to attack frequently, sometimes twice a week. Paul used to have them. Now he was gone, and I had the headaches. Often one would start at work. The fluorescent lights would pulse, and I'd hear myself snapping at people around me. Within two hours I'd be throwing up. I got medication, but it only helped if I could sit in silence and darkness for half a day.

Work became increasingly difficult.

That anniversary month, the church invited me to a four week session on dealing with grief and loss. The minister had been so helpful when Paul died that I felt obligated to go. The first night I looked around the room. There were twenty-five of us. I was one of the youngest, by thirty years. The leader welcomed us and began to speak. He had statistics, quotations, charts. Despite this formal approach, I felt tears well up in my eyes almost immediately. My throat grew hot and tight. Fortunately there were boxes of tissues everywhere. I seized a box and wedged it between my thigh and the armrest of the couch. No one else looked even remotely moved. The leader talked on. Now he was quoting the Bible. I couldn't see a wastepaper container anywhere. By the time a break for tea was announced, a mound of damp, crumpled tissues lay between me and a tiny, beautifully dressed lady next to me on the couch. She leaned toward me, looking concerned.

"Dear, are you getting a cold?"

"No." I scooped up the mountain of tissues in both hands and dumped them in the washroom. In the cubicle I scrubbed my face with toilet paper. Why was I the only one in tears? What was wrong with me?

During the break, one of the survivors suggested a Bereavement Bowling Night. I wanted to hurl my cup and saucer against the window and scream like a banshee.

I never went back.

That spring I sold my desk and took over Paul's study. My own study became a reading room and guest room with a pullout couch for guests I never invited. On nights when my dreams woke me I would huddle on the couch under the blue duvet I'd bought for Paul.

When school ended, my migraines eased almost immediately. The first year anniversary of Paul's death was September. It would be better then. Everyone said so.

September was hell. I was the exception to the rule. My

migraines got worse. The hectic rash that had first appeared at the funeral home returned. I developed arthritis in my left foot.

In desperation I applied for a one semester leave of absence. I said goodbye to Bill. Enough therapy. It wasn't working anyway. Six months off work would make a real difference.

CHAPTER 11

On Leave

A t Christmas that year, my cousin Kate sent invitations to her wedding in Scotland in February. She was marrying a Canadian man she had met while living in the Findhorn Foundation.

"What is this place?" I asked my father.

"Some kind of *spiritual community*," he said, making it sound positively sinister. "I don't like this. Go over and check it out in case you need to stop the wedding."

"Dad, Kate's thirty-four. Old enough to know what she wants." Despite his growls, I declined the wedding invitation. Scotland in February held no appeal though I thought I might visit Kate in June. I had other plans for the winter.

Winter was my favourite time of year now. Paul had always hated the cold and persuaded me to go south for holidays. But I loved cold weather. Skiing was something we'd never done together, and it made me feel alive. I had to stay in the moment when I skied. If I didn't, I fell. There was no past, no future and no messy emotion. With time off work, I went to Gray Rocks, a ski resort near Mont Tremblant in Quebec, for a week. We had group lessons morning and afternoon. My group was assigned to a Level 4 instructor, the highest qualification Canadian Ski Instructors can have. The first time I watched him ski down ahead of me I thought of poetry. He skimmed the snow, he swooped, he flew, light as a snowflake down the white hill, as if there were no ruts, no bumps, no other skiers. I caught my breath at the beauty of it. A moment earlier he had been an arrogant, Quebecois separatist. On skis, he was magic. I wanted to ski like that.

For a week I skied better and faster than I ever had before. Skied way above my usual level.

"Dance, Leslie, dance with the snow," he bellowed and my feet swiveled beneath my body down the steep slope. I fell in love with snow, with skiing, with the exhilaration of speed. When I went home on Saturday, I drove as if I were skiing: light, airy and fast.

I ignored my wedding anniversary in March.

For four months, I skied, I travelled, but I couldn't escape. Every time I slowed down, grief caught up with me. Every time I met my father's kind, concerned and disappointed gaze, I knew he thought I had failed to put Paul behind me, failed to get control of my life.

In June I went at last to Scotland to visit Kate and her new husband in the Findhorn Foundation, east of Inverness. Kate had made a reservation for me at a bed and breakfast in Findhorn Village, a tiny windswept fishing community on the edge of Moray Firth. The window in the living room overlooked Findhorn Bay. Boats lay at anchor, noses into the tide. A forest of black spruce darkened the far shore. The light was very clear. This far north, it doesn't get really dark in June. Paul and I had visited England and Scotland on our last trip together three years before, and I'd loved the light in June. Now it made me uneasy.

Kate bicycled out to meet me, her cheeks red with the wind off the bay, her hazel eyes bright. She was alone; her husband Evan had had an accident on his bike the day before and was at home in bed. Kate and I walked on the beach together, and she told me about her wedding.

"It was a community celebration. All the women walked me to the sanctuary and the men led in Evan. Afterwards we ate dinner in the community centre and danced in the hall. Everyone came, old, young, children, babies. We felt celebrated by the entire community." Her eyes looked starry. Eventually she added, "If you want to learn what this community is about, you should do a couple of work shifts."

I wasn't remotely interested in community, but I didn't say so.

It was obviously important to her.

The next morning I stood on the beach, watched the sailboats in Findhorn Bay move in the current like a school of fish, and remembered the blaze of excitement on Paul's face the day he'd told me he'd put a deposit on a sailboat.

"An Alberg 30. The owner's a widow, remarrying a man with a boat of his own. She wants to sell it quickly before their adult children start to squabble over it so I had to act. Wait till you see it. I'll take you down this weekend. Basic, but really clean lines ..."

It was named Gormay. The widow told me that her husband had been Gord and her name was May. "And we're both good cooks."

I smiled politely.

"Gormay! What a wretched name," I said to Paul in bed that night, flipping through my copy of *The Tempest*. "What about 'Sea Change'? From Shakespeare. Listen:

'Full fathom five thy father lies:
Of his bones are coral made:
Those are pearls that were his eyes;
Nothing of him that doth fade,
But doth suffer a sea-change
Into something rich and strange.'"

I kissed his ear. He looked around suspiciously. "Let me see that. 'Full fathom five thy father lies'? That man's drowned. The ship's wrecked. No. I don't think so." He rolled over and pinned me, knocked *The Tempest* to the floor, kissed my neck. I wriggled.

"He's not dead, he comes back but he's changed. It's the transformative power of-"

"No. No shipwrecks." We both began to laugh.

He loved that boat, spent hours polishing the hull, oiling the teak. We never did change the name.

The sailboats blurred as tears stung my eyes. It was 1992, Paul was dead and I was drowning.

Kate worked full time in the Findhorn Foundation accounts office but she arranged to take an afternoon off the next day to show me around.

The Foundation was a collection of shabby trailers or caravans, a few newer wooden buildings, a stunning Universal Hall, sanctuary and Community Centre, all connected by a network of pretty gardens. The people I saw looked cheerful, but they reminded me of the trailers, worn and shabby. I met Evan at their caravan. He had blue eyes, thick curly salt and pepper hair and a warm smile, despite the pain he was in. Apparently he'd hit a ditch and sailed off the bike into a fence.

Since Evan was out of order and Kate working, I did sign up for a couple of work shifts. I spent a morning in Park Garden. It felt as if I'd stepped into another world. I met eleven people at 9 a.m., and we stood in a circle to say our names. All the others were either members of the community who worked in the garden or guests there on one of the programs. They came from everywhere, the U.S., Germany, England, France, South Africa, Japan. I lost track. I was the only one on a day visit and the only Canadian. We had to hold hands and close our eyes while the person in charge invoked a *garden angel*. I reminded myself it was only one shift. I ended up weeding couch grass out of a hedge with a woman of the community. She was English, about my age, and she told me that her partner had recently left her for another woman in the community.

"It happens a lot here," she said, tears streaking her cheeks. "I just didn't think it would happen to me. I see them all the time, and they look so happy together. I feel as if I should be invisible, as if I'm an embarrassing reminder to them."

I nodded and tried to look sympathetic but I felt impatient. I was a complete stranger. What was I supposed to do with this confidence? I didn't want it. She embarrassed me, she must have embarrassed her ex. He deserved it maybe, but I didn't.

"At least they aren't in the garden group," I said, trying to be helpful. Big mistake. Apparently he *was* one of the garden group. She broke down. I wanted to be anywhere else.

The kitchen shift the next day was better. At least I was prepared for the hand-holding and the angel, kitchen, this time. Eight of us prepared a lunch of soup and salads for one hundred and fifty people. I chopped onions, peeled carrots and washed lettuce with an American man who was there for Experience Week, the starter program. He'd come with his girlfriend, and at the end of the workshop they were going to be married in the sanctuary. He was so excited he could hardly wash the lettuce.

"Imagine, we'll be married here, in the sanctuary," he said, his eyes glowing. "What a start to the marriage."

"Yes, yes, lovely," I said, but he wasn't listening. Just as well. If he'd paid any attention at all he'd have seen I thought him mad.

What I did like was the Phoenix, the general store near the entrance to the Park. It had a terrific book section: health, religion, astrology, Tarot, psychology, philosophy, therapy, plus fiction and poetry. I spent hours there. I also picked up a brochure of the Foundation programs. I was intrigued by one called *The Game of Transformation*, which held out hope of "understanding and transforming key life issues." It sounded a lot easier and faster than therapy. I had a lot of key life issues that needed help. How threatening could a board game be?

On my last night Kate and I ate fish and chips in Findhorn Village, and later we wandered along the beach that faced out to the Moray Firth. The sun hung above the horizon, the water was a calm slate blue and the far shore unbelievably green.

"Are you happy here, Kate? You and Evan could be living in Canada."

"Oh yes, we're happy. We'll return to Canada at some point, but living here is exciting. It's a place of transformation. All that Foundation land used to be like this beach, just sand dunes and gorse. Now it's a garden. "

"And are you – transformed?" She was eight years younger than I was, and I realized I hardly knew her.

She laughed. "I'm a work in progress. We never really stop, do we?"

I didn't answer. I'd nearly stopped. All I wanted was to go backwards.

"The thing is, you can't run away here. Your issues surface, whatever they are, whatever you've been avoiding, and you have to confront them. That's what brings about change."

I don't know what she saw on my face but she put an arm around my shoulders and we walked back to my bed and breakfast without talking much.

You can't run away here. I didn't know whether I heard a threat or a promise.

CHAPTER 12

Body Therapy

My research on the Findhorn Foundation revealed that one of the three founders, Dorothy Maclean, was Canadian, that she, along with Eileen and Peter Caddy had ended up out of work and living, with the Caddys' three young sons, in a trailer park near Findhorn Village in the early 1960s. They established a vegetable garden to supplement their diet and used "guidance" obtained through daily meditation to grow unusually large vegetables in spite of the sandy soil. They called it "co-creation with Nature." Sceptics and scientists tried and failed to find a logical explanation for the size of the vegetables. Over time, a small, diverse community grew. In the mid-1970s, the Experience Week program was developed as a way to introduce guests to the community and its principles. By 1992, the Findhorn Foundation, as it was called, had become one of the oldest and most respected New Age communities in the world and hosted thousands of visitors a year.

Big vegetables. This was so bizarre that the weirdness I'd encountered during my visit seemed almost reasonable. So what if it didn't make sense. Less and less in my life was making sense. I remembered the promise of the Game of Transformation, "to understand and transform key life issues." Unfortunately Experience Week seemed to be a pre-requisite for everything else, and I could only afford one workshop per summer. I ground my teeth and decided to apply to do Experience Week in July the following year. At least I'd see Kate and Evan again.

In September I returned to work in the library. The migraines started again in October.

"Your back is very tight." Alreta's hands lifted my right shoulder as I lay on the massage table. "I cannot feel any give in these muscles. Breathe into this area where my hands are, and see if it will soften."

I rolled my eyes. A rigid, locked-in set of upper back and shoulder muscles was my standard condition.

Alreta was my body therapist. According to her, we hold all our life traumas in the body. She'd put her hand lightly under some part of me as I lay on a massage table and try to move it gently, reminding me to stay neutral. I found it difficult to give up control. At least the treatment wasn't painful. She waited, I breathed obediently, the shoulder moved a little and eventually she shifted to my left shoulder.

"They feel as if they carry the weight of the world. What image comes to you when you think of the right shoulder?"

"I don't know ... a shield, I guess."

"Protection?"

"Yeah, protection. My shoulders have my back, you know?"

"Do you need this?"

"I'm a teacher; teachers need to be alert all the time. Even in the library, you have to know what's going on behind you."

"Why not let the shoulder speak?"

"Why would my shoulder have anything to say? I'm the one in charge."

"Perhaps. But you are having trouble allowing the shoulder to relax, to move. That suggests that you are not as in charge as you think."

I thought the whole point of body therapy was to make the body understand that I was in charge, not some remote body part. But I took a deep breath and waited. The words emerged in my mind.

"She's vulnerable; I'm the protection. I tighten up any time there's a threat," the right shoulder mumbled in my voice.

"What kind of threat?" Alreta asked.

"Whatever upsets her."

"Ah, you're protecting her heart."

"She's afraid of her heart being touched. Too much feeling. She can't cope."

My shoulder was obviously a nutter. But tears began to clog my throat and fill my sinuses. Every time some damned body part found its voice, I'd dissolve. Extraordinary. The only good news was that I was always more relaxed when I left Alreta's office. The bad news was I felt increasingly embarrassed.

In an effort to appease the body and reduce the headaches, I had monthly massages with Craig, who was short and fair-haired, with blue eyes. Although he didn't really look like Paul, there was a superficial resemblance. He had great hands. I needed to be touched, but somehow I couldn't let anyone do that unless I paid them. After Craig left, I would lie in a hot bath, my neck and shoulders aching from the knots he'd uncovered, and yearn for Paul.

I looked forward to the snow, to skiing, to weekends of the one season I didn't associate with Paul. If only I could have lived in permanent winter.

CHAPTER 13
Experience Week

On a cool Saturday in July I got out of the taxi at Cluny Hill College, the Forres campus of the Findhorn Foundation. I stood still for a moment, looking about. Cluny was a large, dignified gray building set into a hill, facing south. Gardens stretched down the hill to a hedge. Beyond that was a narrow lane and a golf course. People were coming and going from the front door, singly and in groups, many hugging each other. As I remembered the embarrassingly emotional people I'd met a year ago when I had visited Kate I felt myself contract. I'd booked this week because I'd felt a flicker of interest a year ago in The Game of Transformation and wanted to see Kate and Evan again. But Kate and Evan had left the Foundation to return to Canada five weeks before I got there, so I was on my own. It was the starter program, Experience Week, I'd signed up for and it looked as if I'd be surrounded by sickeningly sensitive strangers. Again. What was I doing here?

The truth was I'd never learned to live for myself. It had been family, or work, or Paul, never me. Now Paul was dead and I was disconnected. The time in the Foundation was my last ditch attempt to seek something that would keep me out of a permanent depression.

Two people greeted me, a forty-something auburn-haired woman named Jeanette and Tony, a beautiful man with black hair and golden hazel eyes, young enough to be one of my students.

"So you're doing Experience Week?" he said, smiling.

"Well, what I really wanted was the Game of Transformation, but I understand Experience Week has to come first."

"No, the Game stands on its own. There's no prerequisite."

I stared. "Really? Well, I guess – I've made a mistake. Can I do the Game instead?"

"Sorry, no. It doesn't run every week. The next one is in August."

How could I have misread the brochure? Been so stupid? Frustration flared inside me. Behind me, other people were waiting. I bit my lip. "Okay, Experience Week. Give me the form."

After I'd finished the paperwork, Jeanette gave me a quick tour. I saw the lounge, dining room, shop and the sanctuary before she showed me the room I'd been assigned. My two roommates hadn't arrived yet.

"We meet in the Beechtree Room at two this afternoon," she said.

I dropped my suitcase on a bed and moved to the six foot high bay window that overlooked the garden and the golf course. Clouds dotted the sky and the sun shone.

At five minutes to two, I came into the Beechtree Room. It, too, had a massive bay window looking south. A circle of chairs stood in the middle of the room, with a pillar candle in a dish of lavender and sweet peas in the centre. There were flowers everywhere at Cluny, obviously from the garden. I sat close to the window. By this time I'd met my roommates, Katherine from France and Edith from Germany. Lunch in the large, sunlit dining room had been soup and salads, depressingly healthy.

Slowly other people filed in and sat, mostly in silence. Jeanette and Tony looked around the group and smiled in welcome.

"Turn your right palm up and your left down," said Jeanette, demonstrating, "and extend them to the people on either side. That way you receive the group energy with your right and pass it on with the left. Hold hands and close your eyes while we attune to the group."

It was familiar from last summer, but it was also so New Age that I bit my lip to keep from growling.

"Experience Week is meant to introduce you to the Foundation and its principles, show you how community develops within the group and give you a chance to explore your own spirituality," Tony said.

I stared down at the floor. I didn't like God, and I didn't feel like exploring the matter. I shifted in my chair, trying to relax my shoulders.

"You'll have opportunities most evenings to share in the group. That's a part of developing community. We encourage openness and transparency. Whatever you feel is fine, as long as you own it, take responsibility for yourself and don't take your moods out on others. We work on unconditional love. That's a path, a discipline, and it's hard, but it's a goal."

Share. Christ. What did I have to share? I couldn't talk about Paul or my loneliness as a widow without crying, which I was not going to do. What else was there? This was a nightmare.

The group was big, twenty-four with Jeanette and Tony, and varied. We ranged in age from eighteen to mid-fifties. There were five men and nineteen women, from a huge range of countries, Japan, Brazil, the United States, South Africa and nearly every European country. I was the only Canadian. Jeanette was Scottish and Tony Italian.

It was a long afternoon. After we'd heard a lot of general information about the place, we introduced ourselves.

"I came to meet my cousin and her husband, who were living here, but they've gone. I wanted to do the Game of Transformation, but made a mistake and I can't. So I'm here, in this group." I looked around the circle. "But I'm sure it will be an interesting week."

There was no program that night so I joined Katherine and Edith for a sauna. Tony had told us that bathing suits weren't needed and we'd find sauna towels in the changing room. Clad in orange towels, we stepped into the small, dim, wood lined sauna.

A woman was just leaving as we entered. A stark naked woman. Three men sat on the higher bench, not wrapped discreetly in their towels, but sprawled carelessly, nakedly, on top of them. I felt my jaw drop. Katherine and Edith scrambled up, sat down cross-legged on their towels and greeted the men cheerfully. For a moment I clutched my towel to me, paralyzed with shock. Then I crept into the shadowy corner of the lower bench, where the temperature was only moderate, drew my knees up to my chin and closed my eyes.

Was this what they meant by transparency?

After perhaps fifteen, lukewarm moments alone on my lower shelf I was considering a hot shower, when one of the men dropped down to my level. He was gleaming with sweat and he was circumcised. I knew just how little Miss Muffet must have felt.

"You are also in Experience Week, ja?" he said. "I am Klaus."

"Umm - Leslie," I said weakly. He smiled.

"I think it will be a goot workshop."

"Umm humm." Nakedness in the context of relationship was one thing; nakedness among strangers was something completely different. I went for the shower.

On Sunday morning we assembled in the sanctuary for an "Angel Meditation."

Tony laid a circle of small cards face down around the candle in the centre of the sanctuary.

"The angel cards represent qualities we all have," he said. "The one you choose will be one to focus on this week."

After a short meditation, I drew one of the cards. *Purification.* The tiny picture on the card showed an angel either sweating profusely or standing under a waterfall, I wasn't sure which. It reminded me of the sauna except the Angel was clothed. What on earth was I supposed to purify?

Later we took a bus over to the Park. This was where Kate and Evan had lived. We had a tour and assembled in the Park sanctuary for what Jeanette said would be a Work Department attunement.

"We ask all Experience Week guests to work in a department for four shifts during the week, as a way of contributing while they are here but also to understand how we connect with Spirit on an everyday basis. Peter Caddy, one of our founders, said that work is love in action, and that's the philosophy we follow."

She looked around the circle. No one spoke.

"We choose our department by attunement, that is, by closing our eyes, going into a meditative space, listening to what is available and allowing a yes to form in our hearts or minds. What department do you feel called to join? It may not be what you want or expect; you may be guided into one for the work but it may also be in order to meet a particular person or have a very specific experience. You can't really know in advance. So feel into the choices and let the answer emerge."

Feel into the choices? I clenched my jaw. Jeanette listed the departments, with the number of people needed in each one. The number of work spaces equaled the number of people in the program. The departments included garden, kitchen, dining room, homecare in both the Park and Cluny. I knew what I wanted. Cluny Garden. I didn't want to have to commute to and from the Park every day and I wanted to be outside. Easy.

We were supposed to keep our eyes shut and raise our hands for the department we felt "called to join." Even before we were told to open our eyes at the end, I knew that more people had been called to Cluny Garden than there were spaces. Many more, as it turned out. Jeanette reminded us to keep an open mind as she took us back into meditation. Ten minutes later, nothing had changed. Perhaps we would like to talk about it? We looked at each other, but no one seemed inclined to speak. I felt a growing impatience to be out of the sanctuary but Jeanette behaved as if there were all the time in the world. Yet another meditation. Fuck it; what does it matter, I thought. I put my hand up for Homecare. I didn't like housework; who does? But I wanted this "attunement" to end. And I did have the Angel of Purification. By the end of this meditation there had been some change but not enough. Jeanette invited the garden "callees" to share what they'd experienced in their meditation. I relaxed and stopped listening. A couple of minutes later the problem was resolved. Other people must have been impatient too. No one looked particularly happy, except Jeanette and Tony.

At dinner that night, the people who'd got into the gardens glanced up when I said I'd make sure the bathroom sinks were good and clean when they came in to wash after their work shifts.

"Pity the bathrooms here aren't quite as famous as the Findhorn Garden," I added.

One woman shifted uncomfortably on her chair and sighed. "You know, I have a garden at home. I thought gardening here might teach me how to improve it, but maybe I'm being selfish. I could switch with you if you really want to garden."

I wasn't used to having someone call my bluff.

"Ignore me. I'm being bloody minded. You go to the garden and enjoy it."

She laughed.

The sauna had only been the first shock. That night a member of the community visited our group for an "Inner Life Sharing." She told us that Eileen Caddy, one of the founders, had heard God talking to her. I stared. When she said she, too, had heard God's voice, I nearly put my head into my hands. Psychotic. The woman looked sane, but she must be delusional. In Toronto, she'd have been locked up. I glanced around at the rest of my group. Everyone appeared to be taking her seriously except for one man who was nodding off. I stayed silent, didn't join in the question session. Only five more days.

It was raining when I woke up Monday morning so I felt quite pleased to be working inside after all. At 9 a.m. I sat in the Homecare office along with Mark and Greta from my Experience Week group and three Homecare members. Mark looked as if he disliked housework as much as I did. Greta, on the other hand, apparently lived to clean. She was Dutch, blond and twenty-six. I wondered if this enthusiasm for cleaning could be cultural.

"Work is love in action and an opportunity to serve God," said the woman in charge. Greta beamed. Mark snorted. He taught computer studies in a college in the English midlands and had been dragged to the Foundation by his girlfriend. I wondered if he, too, was counting the days. When he set off to vacuum the east and west stairs, he slapped headphones over his ears. Hard rock throbbed as he walked away. The focaliser looked after him thoughtfully. I smiled.

I could have chosen to clean the lounge, but the bathrooms loomed large and I gave in, figuring if I did them Monday morning I could dodge them with a clear conscience for the rest of the week. Someone gave me a blue box of cleaning materials and pointed me to the second floor. I stood in the middle of a large bathroom, staring at the toilet. One floor below me, Greta was also cleaning bathrooms, probably with love. I picked up the toilet brush.

By the end of the morning I had cleaned five bathrooms on the second floor, feeling more like a martyr than anything else. Cluny seemed to be nothing but bathrooms. God required a lot of service.

That afternoon we met in the ballroom for "Community Building Games." I arrived early and sat in one of the window seats to wait for the others. Like the dining room, the ballroom had massive windows on three sides and a high ceiling. The rain from the morning had stopped, and sunshine poured through the stained glass panels at the top of the windows, leaving splotches of green, rose and lilac on the wooden floor. A grand piano and a sound system stood in the corner but otherwise the huge room was empty of furniture. The group drifted in in twos and threes, talking about their work departments. Two Findhorn members, Niels and Heather, called us into the familiar, hand-holding circle to "attune" to the new activity.

I was tired, and I'm not really a games player. Cautiously neutral at best. But it started with learning names, twenty-six now, which was okay. After that there was a series of games that ranged from the simple to the silly. We danced until the music stopped, formed groups of three and gave one word or one sentence answers to personal questions such as, what do you most like about yourself, or, what's something no one here knows about you. We played "hug tag," in which the safe place was in a hug with another person.

"No more than five seconds per hug to be fair to the person who is It," Heather said. "The purpose is to hug as many different people as you can."

I might have balked at that, I'm not one for promiscuous hugging, but it's hard when the whole group starts running and hugging. I got caught up in it before I could help myself.

There were a couple of trust games. My favourite was one in which everyone was blindfolded and assigned an animal. We had to move around making the sound of that animal until we'd found our "family." I was a cow. The ballroom rang with the sounds of mooing, barking, baaing, and oinking as we fumbled about with our hands outstretched. I giggled so much that my moos were inaudible. It was a miracle the other cows found me.

After tea break the games became non-verbal and more serious. We were blindfolded again to explore the hands of a silent, blindfolded, anonymous other, following Niels' directions. In the final game we moved around the room to music, our eyes shut, imagining we were planets circling through a vast universe. Slowly we began to connect with each other until we ended up close together in one big group, swaying like a large, pulsating jellyfish.

By the end of the afternoon, I had had physical contact with every other person in the group. The organizers pulled us back into a circle on the floor and gave us a chance to "share." Back to the New Age. I cringed. But the youngest one in the group beamed around the circle.

"That was fun, I feel much closer to everyone now."

"It is good to know the names," said Klaus, the circumcised man from the sauna.

Edith's eyes were liquid. "I am divorced for three years now. No physical contact. This hug tag game is so good. I like it."

"The afternoon was fun but I had trouble with the blindfolds in the hand exploration game," said Helen, an older American. "I was sexually abused as a child and, well, I was really glad I was put with a woman for that game. I could tell it was a woman because Katherine's hands are so small."

There was an extended silence, broken at last by Rick, a gorgeous, blue-eyed blond in his twenties. "Yeah, thanks for saying that, Helen. I'm bi-sexual. I always wonder if it's safe to tell people but in this group, it feels okay."

I sat like a stone, shocked silent. How could people speak so intimately about themselves?

My modus operandi usually involves watching a group until I feel I've got the measure of it before I speak. But this was way out of my usual league. I couldn't get the measure of anyone. That night after dinner, another community member joined the group for a Nature Sharing. I'd read about the Foundation principle of "co-creation with Nature," in which Dorothy Maclean meditated and got advice on growing large vegetables. But somehow that hadn't prepared me for this man saying he'd seen a "Nature Spirit" in the garden. Hearing voices *and* seeing things! If I hadn't been so tired after Homecare and the Community Building Games, I might have felt panicky. As it was, I looked around the circle searching for skepticism that matched my own and didn't see it. Did no one but me have a grasp of consensus reality?

I didn't share that night either.

As I worked in Homecare Tuesday morning, scrubbing the sauna bench with hot water and soap, I thought about the week so far. It was nearly half way through and I hadn't spoken much at all. Jeanette and Tony didn't pressure anyone, but I could feel the eyes of the others in the group, wondering what was wrong with me.

Somewhere between cleaning the first and second sauna bench, I remembered the Pine River Multicultural Leadership week when I'd met Paul. Paul and I had led one of the student groups during this five day residential workshop. On Day One, I realized I couldn't hide behind my role of teacher. Out of role I was nervous and vulnerable. But that week changed my life, and not just because I met Paul. I had to stand my ground in a group as a real person. Only the courage of the students had enabled me to get through it.

The program involved speaking from the heart, not a lesson plan. There were no experts. The students were nearly all immigrants and knew a lot more about survival than I did. I had no desk between me and them. I'd been in tears frequently - me, logical, analytical, unemotional and pragmatic me. I remembered Jackie, the student who'd stayed most vividly in my mind.

"I'm fat," she'd said, looking around the group. "I know that's not a strength but in my school, if you're fat you've only got two choices: go under, give up and drop out, or get stronger and survive. I'm a survivor. All the women in my family are like me: big, fat and strong. I'm strong *because* I'm fat. I was scared starting high school but my mom said straight out – you gotta face it. You're bright, you've got terrific ideas and you work hard. If those kids can't see that – and they may not, it's a weird age – you have to keep going forward until people around you do see it. Your body is big, okay – but your mind and your soul are way bigger.

"I was scared coming here. My teacher recommended me because I am a leader, even though she knows and I know, no one in my class wants a fat leader. They'd rather have somebody skinny and pretty whether she's got brains or not. But I'm here and you've all made me feel like I'm worth it."

I'd never admired anyone as much as Jackie that day.

I scrubbed the second wooden bench, soaking my jeans in the process. Had I learned nothing from that Leadership Week? From Jackie? I had committed to Experience Week; I had to get something out of it. If sharing was what it took, I'd share. Time to test the waters of openness and transparency. I filled the bucket again and flung clean hot water over the benches, washing away the soap.

That night in the group I cleared my throat after someone else had finished a rhapsody about the garden.

"This -" I waved my hand around to indicate the group and all of Cluny - "isn't what I'm used to. It's a big learning curve. Jeanette told me earlier today that the British love eccentrics. Canadians aren't so comfortable with them. I think we're more inhibited. Well, I am. The first shock was the sauna, Saturday night. In Canada, we – well, I've never been in a sauna naked with strangers of both sexes. It didn't seem to bother anyone else so I guess my assumptions about men and nakedness are maybe – just my assumptions. Not necessarily true." I glanced around the group. The Americans smiled understandingly at me, the British looked poker-faced and everyone else seemed puzzled.

"Anyway, today in Homecare I volunteered to clean the sauna. I attuned to my angel of Purification and imagined all of you in there with me. Naked. I think it helped."

Startled laughter bubbled up in the circle.

"The next sauna night is tomorrow, and it's our free evening. I'll be there about 7:30, naked, and I hope you'll all come and join me. The sauna is beautifully clean."

About half of them did come. I climbed up to the second level, having practised several times on Tuesday, sat nude and cross-legged on my towel in the heat and beamed. I could see their teeth gleam as they grinned back. My first step into the New Age at last.

Mark had not come. Like me, he was struggling with the place. During an afternoon sharing, he exploded.

"This place is fucking unreal. Nobody is this accepting all the time. I don't believe it." His face was red and the veins in his neck bulged. No one spoke. Jeanette and Tony looked interested but neither alarmed nor upset. For a few minutes Mark glared around the circle. People looked steadily back at him. I noticed a few grins. Only his girlfriend, Bel, seemed angry. When he caught her eyes, Mark deflated like a burst balloon.

"Sorry, I'm bringing you all down, I know I'm too negative, I just ... I can't ..."

"Don't bleat, Mark," said one of the women. "There's nothing wrong with what you've said if it's what you feel."

"Be cool, man," said an American. "I've wondered about that too. Maybe some people are trying too hard, but I actually think there is a lot of acceptance here. Maybe we're just not used to it."

We broke for tea then. To my own surprise, I hugged Mark on my way out of the room. He leaned into me gratefully. I felt so much better after listening to him, though I couldn't think why.

During the Friday morning Homecare shift I felt the unmistakable symptoms of migraine. Awful timing. I couldn't miss the Completion session Friday afternoon. At lunch I took double the usual medication. But when we met at 2 p.m., I had to sit with my back to the bay window and the others looked blurred around the edges.

Tony pulled out a stone he'd picked up during our trip to the beach last Sunday to use as a "talking stone" for the completion sharing.

"This is your opportunity to say whatever you need to say before we complete our time together as a group. During the meditation, I'll remind us what we've done this week. Afterwards I'll open the space for sharing. Use the stone and then pass it on to someone else when you're done." He glanced around, then invited us to close our eyes.

I sent up a silent prayer for the bloody headache to let go. By the time the meditation had finished, however, I felt the familiar queasiness and knew that I had better speak now. I picked up the stone, cool and heavy in my hand.

"I want to go first because I have a bad headache and might not last the afternoon." I drew a deep breath. "When Mark said that not everyone was as accepting as we seemed to be, he could have been talking about me. I've found this week hard, because of the level of honesty ... no, it's really intimacy - that seems to be a norm here. Intimacy in a relationship I can cope with; intimacy with a bunch of strangers is – has not been what I'm used to or comfortable with. I'm grateful you said what you did, Mark; it helped me to know someone else questioned it here. It's easier for me to – well, to take my clothes off than to show how vulnerable I am. I have this need to be seen as strong and in control but I'm not a lot of the time and it's hard for me to accept that, never mind let it show.

"Thank you all for being so patient with my silence, while I found my voice. It helped. I hope I can take some of the acceptance home with me."

I forced myself to focus as I looked around at them. They were smiling. I handed the stone to Mark, then closed my eyes and listened as the others shared. After a few minutes, I found, to my astonishment, that the headache was receding.

"This week was nothing like I thought it would be. I don't feel as sure about home now or myself. I think I might have changed. I didn't expect that."

"The place is great, and you all were a good time too. I loved being in the Park Kitchen. I've never seen a group of guys 'cooking with love' before."

"I'll take more of a Findhorn approach to my children now, I think, after having the Angel of Love for the week. More accepting, less critical. Maybe I'll even send them for an Experience Week."

"I take home Eileen Caddy book on guidance. Use. Thank you for patient with my bad English. You all beautiful peoples."

You all beautiful peoples. My eyes were wet.

I still wasn't sure about sharing or the Foundation, but I said goodbye with real affection to my roommates and to Mark and Greta and the focalisers before I left for a retreat on the island of Iona on the west coast. The Foundation had a house there, called Traigh Bhan.

It was a small one and a half story building set in a sloping, east-facing field in the middle of a farm. A stone wall separated the house and its wild, luxuriant garden from the sheep and cows. The glassed-in front porch faced the Iona Strait and the island of Mull. The sea was blue, or gray or silver, depending on the weather. The clouds changed from moment to moment, the tides shifted and seals and sea birds appeared and disappeared, as did the rainbows. A host and five other guests stayed there as well. Because it was a retreat, we were mostly on our own. I wrote about

Experience Week in my journal, meditated in the sanctuary with its views in three directions, walked the hills, fascinated by the ever changing light, and every night I climbed Dun I, the highest point of the island, to watch the sun set far out in the Atlantic. I felt peaceful and centred, almost happy.

One night after I'd gone to bed, I remembered that I, too, had heard a voice the day after Paul had died, telling me not to commit suicide. I sat up in bed. Moonlight splashed onto the floor, silver in the blackness. When Paul died I might have been unbalanced but surely I hadn't been psychotic. I wasn't spiritual either. But if I was neither mad nor spiritual – *did* ordinary people hear voices? Maybe consensus reality wasn't as obvious as I'd assumed it to be.

By the end of the week, I thought I might return to the Foundation next year after all and play the Game of Transformation.

CHAPTER 14
Ashes to Ashes

I felt so much better when I got home from the two weeks in Scotland that I wondered if I could finally scatter Paul's ashes. I'd hugged strangers; I'd been naked with strange men. I'd even been vulnerable and honest in front of a group of people. I'd had a headache disappear just when it seemed to be getting worse. Surely I was strong enough. If I could let go of his ashes, I could commit fully to life without him at last. The ashes had been sitting in the box on a bookshelf in Paul's study ever since my sister had picked them up a month after the funeral. Nearly four years.

A long time ago, just after his father's death, Paul and I had talked about cremation and the scattering of ashes. We were in bed at my place, drinking tea after making love.

"I'd like my ashes scattered in places where I have been really happy, when the time comes," he had said. "Japan - but that's obviously off limits. Too far."

"No kidding. You can just scatter me in Georgian Bay. Anywhere. It's the most beautiful place in my world."

"Let's see, there's a park where Bev and I used to go camping every weekend in the spring and fall ..."

"You think I'm going to scatter your ashes someplace where you spent happy times with your wife? You must be mad. I can't even get you to divorce her," I said without heat. "Think again."

He laughed. "Okay, okay. What about Leslie's Cove? On the shore, not in the water."

I blinked. Leslie's Cove was the name he had given to a small protected bay where we'd once swum naked and then made love on the sun-warm rocks. I smiled, turned toward him and kissed him.

"Yeah, I could do that."

On a sunny summer day in August I drove north. It took three hours to reach the stony beach on the edge of Lake Huron where Paul and I had begun our hike ten years earlier. I scrambled along the Bruce Trail for another two hours looking for the little bay, but the landscape had changed. Trees had fallen or grown; the shoreline looked unfamiliar. I searched and searched, but I couldn't find the place. I sat down at last on a high rocky ledge and remembered wonderful days hiking, camping, sailing and swimming in our eight years together. It doesn't matter if I don't have the exact cove, I told myself. I'm up here, in the area, remembering Paul, remembering us. I held the container of ashes in my lap. A warm wind blew through the forest of green pines, cedars and poplars below me. The water shone blue and restless beyond the trees. I closed my eyes for a while, the sun warm on my skin. At last I opened the black plastic box. Froze.

What I wanted ... what I really wanted was to strip off my clothes, lie naked on the rocks in the sunshine and upend the box of gritty grey granules over me, inhaling the dust, absorbing the grit. I wanted him, on top of me, inside me, in my hair and eyes and in every sweaty crease of my body. I wanted to roll in what was left of him so thoroughly that his essence could never be washed away. I wept, convulsed with grief as raw as it had been a month after his death.

Nearly an hour later I calmed down enough to tip the ashes into the trees below me. They floated down and vanished into the green sea. I put the black box into my backpack with shaking hands and began the long hike back.

CHAPTER 15

The Game of Transformation

cceptance might work in the Findhorn Foundation but not in my life in Toronto. The unexpected tide of grief over the ashes cancelled out any benefit from my two weeks in Scotland. Depression, headaches and exhaustion from teaching and library work dragged me down further. Only the promise of ski season sustained me. I spent long hours at the gym getting fit for winter. But ski season in Ontario only lasted three months. By the time I'd returned from a March Break ski holiday out west, the hills north of Toronto were bare. I booked my flight to Scotland and endured another three months of endless, depression-grey days before the summer holidays began at last.

This time I'd finally get to play the Game of Transformation, the workshop that promised hope for "understanding and transforming key life issues." I needed rescue. I needed to be free of grief. Therapy and massage weren't doing it. I needed a magic pill.

"The Game of Transformation is a board game that we use as a tool for change," said Judith, one of the two Game Guides for our small group. She beckoned the five of us toward a white, circular table about three and a half feet in diameter, the board on which we would play the next day. Thin black lines divided the table into five curving pie-shaped paths, one for each player. In the centre was a small circle. Both the circle and the paths were made up of small squares.

"Each of you plays with two purposes, which shape your game. One is a receiving purpose, what you hope to get from the game;

the other is a giving purpose, a quality you contribute to the game, such as honesty or openness. Both purposes need to be succinct and clear. Tonight after dinner you five will meet as a group to share your two purposes. Because we all support each other during the game, it is essential that you understand everyone's purpose, the background, why it is important. What other players learn from their games is also in some way your lesson. You mirror for each other."

My eyes flickered from the board to her face and back.

"What is all that?" asked Lisa from Italy, pointing to decks of cards, markers, boxes of small cardboard pieces that sat nearby.

"The various bits," Judith said. "The Game is very complex. You don't need to worry about the rules; Joshua and I handle all the logistics; that's our role. We keep a record and we channel the energy of the spirit of the Game."

I hesitated for a moment at the thought of "channelling the energy," then relaxed. I'd come to terms with the idea in Experience Week the year before and Judith and Joshua looked the essence of sanity. Judith was slight, serene and quiet. Joshua was an immense man with coke-bottle thick glasses over blue eyes and an edge in his voice that suggested he did not tolerate fools gladly. But his chief function was to record the events of the game, and Judith did most of the talking.

"Tomorrow morning you meet with Joshua and me in our Game room and give us a short version of your purposes and the background. Then we begin play. But remember, for you the Game has already started. The energy continues throughout the week, not just as you move your markers around the board. You are also in the Game energy during tea breaks and meals, at night, in dreams, waking and sleeping."

Years later, someone explained to me that the Game of Transformation represents the essence of the Findhorn Foundation concentrated into a one week workshop. The same energy, the same kind of experience, the essential confrontations that will enable someone to transform their major issues, if they have the courage and honesty and willingness to stay with it. It was certainly no magic pill. But maybe I needed to see it that way then.

I'd been clear about my receiving purpose for a year. *I intend to release my husband, my marriage and my grief and move on.* I couldn't be more succinct than that. After dinner that evening, I climbed the stairs to the sun room to meet the other players and talk about purposes, and wondered what Paul would have made of the Findhorn Foundation. Not much, probably. He wasn't interested in spirituality or community, and he didn't talk publicly about his feelings. He just - was. For a moment I longed for him so badly I had to stop climbing and lean against the banister to stay standing.

The five of us gathered in the small, glassed in porch, our faces pink in the setting sun. I'd felt secure with Judith and intimidated by Joshua. I was much less sure how I felt about my playing group. We were five women, four of us in our forties and the fifth in her early twenties. We came from the U.S., Germany, Italy, Belgium and Canada. There was a long silence before I offered to speak first. I started as I meant to go on. Clear, factual and brief.

"I've been a widow for nearly five years but I'm still feeling grief-stricken at worst, numb at best. I hope the Game will help unstick me from grief and loss so I can live again. I intend to release my husband, my marriage and my grief and move forward. I plan to bring my sense of humour to the game as a giving purpose."

They asked a few questions about Paul that I answered briefly, clamping down hard on my feelings. If I started all weepy I'd never move anywhere.

But that was me. Irma from Germany cried all the way through her purpose description, which seemed to take forever. I felt my whole body tighten as I gripped my patience and endured. Alice, the American, was afraid of being overheard; she spoke so softly I tried to read her lips. The higher the two of them registered on the sensitivity scale, the more irritable I felt. It was a relief to listen to Lisa, who was direct and straightforward.

The twenty-something woman, Anna from Belgium, shared last. She told us that she was psychic, could pick up our internal thoughts and moods almost at once on her inner radar and felt little need of speech. I was fascinated and bubbled over with questions, but Anna cut me off.

"To be psychic is not a game. The information is sometimes overwhelming. It also sets me apart, makes me a freak. I would rather be like everyone else. I have spent much time trying to be normal but it does not work. Mental institutions are filled with people like me."

I shut up.

It took three and a half hours to complete our purpose work, and I was so exhausted by the end that I fell asleep as soon as my head hit the pillow. No dreams.

The next morning we met Judith and Joshua in our Game area, a low, white building on the edge of the woods behind Cluny. It was very quiet. The scent of cedar and pine drifted in the open windows with the sunshine.

Once we'd reviewed our purposes and put our markers in the circle at the centre of the playing table, Judith told us that we needed to roll the die until we landed on a birth square and only then would we move onto our individual life paths.

"The Game is played on several levels and the first one is physical. As you gain in experience and awareness you move up to other levels," she explained. "Emotional, mental, intuitive and so on. Not everyone plays on every level. Sometimes a person stays mostly on one, sometimes they move quickly to new ones.

"As you travel around the life path, every square you land on, every card you draw, is meant to deepen in some way your understanding of the issue and of yourself. Our questions are to help you do that as well," she said. "If you are open to it, we'll give you feedback occasionally, with your permission. You go as quickly or as slowly as you want. We do not push each other or try to fix anyone. We accept; we allow. Whatever you feel is your choice."

She invited us all to choose a "Guardian Angel" card, a quality that would support us with our purposes during the game. The little angel on my card lay on her stomach, her chin in her hand, reading. *Understanding.* I beamed.

"Understanding is perfect. I love to read and I'm quick to pick up what I need to know," I told them.

"Understanding from the heart is such a strength," said Anna, and the others nodded. I stiffened slightly. The heart? I must have looked bewildered because Joshua put down his pen and spelled it out to me in his rumbling bass voice.

"Your purpose is to release grief for your husband. Clearly this is a heart issue. Understanding is of the heart as well as of the mind and spirit."

My face fell. He raised one eyebrow and his mouth twitched.

We started to play. Irma and Lisa were born almost immediately but I kept missing the birth square. By mid-morning only Anna and I remained unborn. Then Irma landed on a Miracle Square and offered to "birth" Anna and me as part of her miracle. Anna was pleased. I wasn't. I didn't like Irma. She was fuzzy minded and emotional, apparently incapable of clear thinking. But she'd been born first, and now she had a miracle.

"Thanks, Irma, but I'd prefer to be born without help," I said stiffly.

By mid-afternoon all the others were having fine times with angels, insights, setbacks, depressions, while I inched around the small pre-birth circle, snarling inwardly while I should have been meditating. Judith eyed me. I knew I was supposed to ask myself whether I was ready to step fully into my purpose, to release Paul. I'd been silently asking the question; I kept answering yes. I'd scattered his ashes, hadn't I? But when nothing changed, I wanted to weep. I told myself I was frustrated and angry.

While I kicked my heels, I watched the others' games. Irma was trying to sort and clear problems she had in relationships in Germany, but she was never able to see the behaviour patterns that caused the trouble. The Game cards she drew brought them up again and again, but each time she was bewildered, often tearful. I tried to shove the box of tissues at her once but Judith stopped me.

No fixing. I bit my lip. Even Insight cards, meant to remind you of your strengths or point out a possible direction, didn't help Irma. Despite gentle feedback from Judith and the rest of us, she couldn't hear it. Extraordinary. How could she be so dim? And she took so long to finish her turn. Everything seemed long to me as I sat, waiting to play.

After the afternoon tea break, I finally spoke out.

"I'm pissed off at myself for turning down your offer of a miracle birth this morning, Irma. I'm fed up with doing nothing and I know I might not get born for days. The worst of it is, it's my own fault."

Everyone grinned. Obviously they had been aware of this for hours. Embarrassed, I threw the die onto the board and stared. My number came up. The marker landed on a birth square. I was born. Grins became laughter.

"Hey! Your angel heard you. Congratulations."

"Well, her giving purpose is humour," Lisa said. "Now we see that the angel has a sense of humour too."

I bit back the swear word on my tongue, accepted the physical level score card from Judith and tried to smile. At least my Game had started at last.

But nothing went right. The more I fought to move forward, the more gluey the whole process felt. I got a number of Setbacks, and at one point I ended up in a Dark Night of the Soul, a kind of major depression in which I was supposed to don sunglasses, retreat inwardly, ignore the process of others and *feel* the isolation. I'd fought my frustration mostly in silence this far, unwilling to admit how difficult I was finding it all, and this Dark Night process seemed like the final straw. My purpose was to release pain, grief and depression. I couldn't understand why I was getting more of it. My Game was as much of a pit as life in Toronto had been for five years. Where was the "magic pill?" Where was the fucking transformation?

Eventually I got out of the Dark Night of the Soul. But one move later, when I got an Insight card that read: "God's will for me is perfect happiness. Blessings all round," I felt even worse. I tried to smile at the others. *God should get his agenda straight. Perfect bloody happiness does not usually involve losing a husband you love within six months of marriage.* I bit my lip to stop the tears.

That night as I was getting ready for bed, one of my room-mates, the American woman, Alice, leaned over and whispered, "Can I give you some feedback?"

Alice's whispering drove me mad. If you aren't going to speak loudly enough so someone can hear you, why bother speaking at all? But I hadn't learned how to say no here and besides, she fixed me with a stare like the Ancient Mariner. I nodded.

"I see you fight back tears every time you speak about Paul. Maybe you should let yourself cry since your feeling is so strong."

"Thank you for sharing," I said, biting back my anger. I was there to let go of grief, not wallow in it. I pulled my duvet over my head and turned my back on her.

Forty minutes later, I was still rigid with fury. My roommates were all breathing deeply and rhythmically. Obviously I wasn't going to fall asleep anytime soon. I got up, pulled on sweat pants, socks and a sweater and headed for the sanctuary.

I knelt down on a cushion, wrapped one of the sanctuary blankets around my shoulders, and lit the candle. The darkness dissolved; in the flickering candlelight the sanctuary became a pleasant, shadowy oasis. It was good to be alone. Slowly I began to relax, and my anger faded.

Eventually I thought about Paul. Remembered the warmth of his body in bed, the companionship of our silences, the shared laughter. I almost never laughed now. I remembered how much he had loved the countryside around the Caledon Inn, the scenery in Georgian Bay, the evening sky at dusk when we'd lit a campfire. Remembered the tea he'd make on Sunday mornings when we would stay in bed, talking, drinking tea and making love, when time seemed to stop for us. Remembered how we'd touch when he was in the hospital, and we talked of ordinary things, of our love, of hope, not illness or fear of separation. Remembered my daily prayer, for the strength to put his needs first, to be his rock, to channel a love as pure and as comforting as God's.

Tears burned my eyes but I blinked them back.

Time passed. I pulled the blanket closer around me.

Eventually I let myself remember what I hadn't been able to bear remembering until now. The day all his tubes were removed to prompt his digestive system to work on its own. His eyes lit up at the thought of his first bath since the surgery some ten days earlier. I ran the water and helped him into the deep hospital tub, washed his hair and his scarred, wasted body while he closed his eyes and sighed in pleasure. But his digestive system shut down. That night they replaced the tubes. When I arrived the next day, his face was shuttered in defeat.

The evening the nurses had taken him back down to the X-ray department. Something in his eyes, fear or despair, made me decide to stay. He'd said that the X-ray department had been so cold that afternoon that he hadn't got warm for hours after. So I peeled off my clothes and climbed into his bed, wearing only a shirt. I was nearly asleep when he came back. He slid into the narrow bed and burrowed into the curves of my body. I held him until he was warm and drowsy. It was midnight when I left. None of the staff said anything.

The time when I was massaging his feet, and he said, without warning, "Do you really think I can get through this?"

My hands stopped moving, my left hand holding his heel, my right thumb still pressed into the arch, the fingers across the top of his foot. I looked into his eyes from the end of the bed. For a moment I didn't speak. Then my mouth opened and someone said: "Yes, I think you can. It will take a miracle and a lot of energy on your part. I believe in miracles, but if you are too tired, if you've been through too much, it's okay. I understand. You decide. I'll be fine."

My voice – the voice – was steady, firm and full of love. I heard it with a kind of wonder. Then he held out his arms for me and I moved up beside him and put my face against his shoulder. We lay still for a long time without speaking.

He died the next night.

I wiped my eyes with the blanket, and the sanctuary came momentarily back into focus.

It wasn't my voice that had given Paul permission. It couldn't have been. I didn't love so unselfishly. I wasn't so strong. But the prayer that I'd prayed twice every day for three and a half weeks, on my way into and out of the hospital, for the strength to put Paul's needs first, to love him as purely as God would love – it must have been the prayer that opened a channel for those words. Hadn't I asked exactly that? *Let me be a channel.* My prayer had been answered. Did I regret it? No. I meant every word of that prayer every time I said it, and I was grateful beyond all words for the way it had been answered.

It was just - "I'm not strong enough without him," I whispered and gave in to the grief I had struggled to repress all week.

The silence in the sanctuary seemed to deepen.

Paul's death had been quick, not prolonged. His doctor had been surprised. But I was sure death came because I had set Paul free to choose, loved him enough to let go.

It was a miracle. Not the one I had longed for but still a miracle. I hugged the certainty to me with the blanket and smiled through my tears.

Then – Paul had been such a good man in every way; wouldn't his death have been a good one regardless of my prayers? What if … what if the miracle was not just for Paul? What if it was for me? I straightened up on my cushion, my fingers kneading the blanket. Anyone, even the angry, old, white man God of my childhood, could love Paul. It was hard to believe that I could merit a miracle. But that prayer, the quality of presence I'd been able to bring to my visits with him, my words – "I'll be fine; do what you need to do" – none of it was the person I had known myself to be all my life.

About four hours after I'd left my bed, I crept back, chilled, cried out and exhausted. I fell asleep immediately.

In the morning I felt drained. When I reached the Game room, the others looked uncertainly at me.

"You seem different," Irma said. "Younger, somehow, softer." Her eyes were warm with concern.

"Are you all right?" whispered Alice.

I nodded. I couldn't seem to speak. Why had I disliked them so much?

In my final move of the Game I took an Insight card and read: "You are radiant with Acceptance." I felt a stillness inside me, as if all forward motion were suspended.

In the Completion sharing I finally found a voice. Tears slid down my face as I talked. No one offered tissues.

"Last night I couldn't sleep. I went to the sanctuary and ... I think I had a real Dark Night of the Soul. And a miracle. Both."

I described what had happened. They leaned forward watching me in absolute silence, their eyes full of compassion.

"I don't really know if this makes sense. I just know it's as important as anything else that's happened to me in the group this week. Now I wonder whether there's another way of living altogether that – somehow – incorporates what I've been through. Whether trying to let go of the grief is the point. Maybe it's not about moving on and putting it behind me but just about accepting everything that's happened." I looked around the group. Joshua's coke bottle glasses had misted over, and he took them off. When he tried to speak his voice broke.

"I think your role in life is to feel and radiate joy. To be able to accept all of life, including the grief, is the first step." He put his enormous hand over mine and squeezed.

CHAPTER 16
Shadow

Normal life is a crash landing after the Game of Transformation.

September came. Migraines, skin rash and arthritis came with it. They never entirely disappeared but they were much less present when I was on holiday. With this in mind, I had signed up for another year off in four years time. Meanwhile I looked forward to winter. Kathleen had persuaded me to sign up for Ski Instructor Training that year, despite my age. I was turning forty-four in November.

"It's just the next step," she said. "Since your weeks in Gray Rocks you've been at the top of the highest class. There's nowhere else for you to go except Instructor Training."

I signed up, but to fight the feeling that I looked too old for Instructor Training, I began to get monthly facials, along with my massages. I might be a mess internally, but I was going to look good.

At Christmas I returned to Gray Rocks for another week of intensive ski instruction. The first night a tall, lean, silver-haired American asked me if I was single.

"I'm a widow," I said, blushing slightly.

"But are you single?"

When I didn't answer, only blushed more deeply, he raised his glass in a toast to me and invited me for a drink in his room the next afternoon. I accepted.

Al and I danced every night that week, my skiing improved, and the romance made me wonder if I was emerging from the long night of grief at last. Being with Al was like skiing. I blotted out the past and the future, didn't think, just focused on the present.

But where skiing made me feel alive in myself, Al was an echo, a reminder of what it felt like to be with someone. Not Paul, just – someone.

I was surprised when he phoned two days after the Gray Rocks week. I had seen him only as a holiday fling. But as flowers, cards and small gifts arrived over the weeks that followed, I thought, well, why not? Al lived in Virginia and worked at a military staff college in Washington, D.C. I wouldn't see him often. One of the gifts he sent me was a deep blue coffee mug with his college crest in gold. I took it into work for my coffee breaks. Tilly, the library clerical worker, teased me about my American Army conquest.

I couldn't summon up any real enthusiasm for work, but it was going smoothly enough now. We'd had cutbacks in Tilly's clerical hours in the fall, but a social worker had shown up about then and persuaded me to accept a volunteer in the library. She explained that Marilyn, the volunteer, was a recluse about my age who had dropped out of school in Grade 9 and pretty much stayed at home ever since. A federal government initiative had been designed to help people like her get back into the work world through a volunteer program. If she got a placement and stuck to it, she'd get a bit more money in her welfare cheque. The plan was to help her acquire a few social skills along with the filing and shelving. It was hard to say no; we needed help. Practically and logically it seemed like a win-win situation.

I did hesitate, though. Marilyn was - odd. She'd said almost nothing when the social worker brought her in, just peered out through a curtain of dark hair. I could see black eyes, crooked, shadowed teeth and a furtive expression but not much more. Her movements were stiff and jerky, like a robot in need of oil. She backed away from the catalogue computers as if they were guard dogs. Jim supervised her, and if she spoke at all, it was to Tilly. I ignored her or tried to. I didn't like the way her black eyes watched me whenever she thought I wasn't looking.

Al phoned a couple of times a week. I wrote to him, which I preferred to the phone. Meanwhile I skied every weekend. Instructor training was going well. I got therapy, massage and facials regularly and told myself I was happy enough.

But the migraines continued.

I always carried the strong pills my doctor had prescribed and took one the moment I registered the odd blurring at the edges of my vision and the instant crankiness that came with it. If I was at school, I'd try to retreat into my office and shut off the lights. If I could stay there half an hour, there was a chance the medicine would work well enough to let me finish the day without vomiting. Jim understood; he'd abandon his computer and deal with the check-out desk when he saw me reach for the pills. Tilly did too, in her own way.

"God, put on some lipstick, your face'll scare the students," was her usual response.

The first time Marilyn saw me reach for water with the pill bottle in my hand, she barked: "What are those pills? Are you on drugs?"

"None of your goddammed business."

Maybe Jim could teach Marilyn social skills. I couldn't. I always wanted to lash out when her black eyes bored into me like x-ray. When I was healthy I could ignore her, but headaches dropped my guard to the point where I snapped. She didn't seem to mind. I couldn't understand why not, and after a while I stopped trying.

Ignoring Marilyn, however, was a mistake. Jim came into my office one morning, shut the door and sat down across from me. I was going over the budget line by line to see what I could squeeze out of it for new atlases. Governments never think about library book budgets when they change the borders and names of their countries. I looked up.

"It's Marilyn," he said. "You probably haven't noticed but she's been extending her hours. She's working five days a week from 9 to 4:00. That's not what you set up originally, is it?"

"No. We said four days from nine till noon, but ..."

"Well, she's doing all Tilly's work, and I don't think that's good. We might run into problems with the union, and we're running the risk of having Tilly's hours cut again, if the Admin team notices."

"Yikes. You're right." I massaged my forehead. "Okay, I'll tell Marilyn she's got to go back to the hours we agreed. Thanks for the warning."

He got up. "You know she's not going to like it?"

We both glanced out at the library, through the windows of my office. Marilyn was shelving in Reference, casting sideways looks at us. Jim and I didn't usually do business behind closed doors.

"I know. You'd better warn Tilly she's going to have more work to do."

I found Marilyn shelving in the science section the next morning. She froze when she saw me coming. I explained the problem as clearly and pleasantly as I could.

"You need to go back to three hours a day, but if you want to volunteer somewhere else in the afternoons, I'll be happy to give you a reference," I finished.

Marilyn straightened her thin shoulders and lashed out.

"I don't remember any agreement. You're lying. You need me. Tilly doesn't like the work," she barked. I stared at her, stunned. My fingers curled into fists.

"I'll call your social worker in. Perhaps that will refresh your memory. But be clear about this, Marilyn. You will not jeopardize the work of a paid staff member."

Two days later Barbara, the social worker, met with me and Marilyn in the library seminar room.

"Marilyn doesn't understand nuance," Barbara had said on the phone. "You'll need to be clear."

I'd show them *clear*. I explained the situation. Marilyn sat, silent and rigid. Barbara confirmed the original agreement and told Marilyn she had to cut back her hours, as requested.

"But - what about what I want?" Marilyn asked her.

"The needs and wishes of the employer take priority. You're a volunteer; you adjust. We discussed this before you started, if you recall."

"I think that's all." I stood up. "Thank you, Barbara."

"Wait," Marilyn said. She stared at me. "I want some time with you. You never spend any time with me."

I stared back. "Time? What do you mean? You have lots of opportunity to see my schedule. I don't have enough time to do my job, I'm not spending it with you. If you've got a question, Jim will answer it. If he can't, I will."

She glowered. "You have coffee breaks. All your conversations with teachers are not about work. And you make private phone calls, sometimes; I've heard you. You've got time, I only want a little each day. I think I deserve it."

She'd been spying on me. I couldn't have been more astonished if a book had bitten me. My voice was glacial when I spoke.

"No. This job obviously isn't working out as you want it to. I'll understand if you decide it's time to leave."

"Are my clothes all right?"

"What? I don't care what you wear as long as you're covered. Do you understand what I've said about the hours?"

Jim rolled his eyes when I told him about the meeting but said little. Marilyn came in the next morning and shelved five books in three hours. At noon, she looked at the trucks of books waiting to be shelved and said she had a little more time, if we needed her.

"Tilly will do the rest, thanks," Jim said. "We'll see you tomorrow."

She stomped out. Tilly laughed. I heaved a sigh of relief.

About this time, Al's phone calls began to change too.

"Tell me more about your work. What are the students like, and the staff in your department? When are you going to come down and see me?"

He didn't want to hear that all my weekends were booked with ski instructor training sessions.

"I'm always calling you; why don't you call me sometimes?"

"I write you. Lighten up Al, please."

Instead of glowing after his calls I was irritable. It wasn't his fault. I should have realized I wasn't interested in any in-depth commitment when I had been glad he lived so far away. But did this mean I was incapable of loving anyone other than Paul? I decided to try harder.

One February weekend I got my Level 1 Ski Instruction certification. I took a week of unpaid leave from school in March to take the Level 2. After floundering for a couple of days, I found my feet, managed to teach a good lesson on short radius turns and passed. I came home just in time to do laundry, repack and take off for Whistler with the ski club at March Break. Al simmered away resentfully back in Virginia, but I promised to see him at Easter.

After two weeks of skiing, I was tired and ready enough to go back to work. There was a definite "atmosphere" in the library that Monday morning. Neither Tilly nor Marilyn was speaking, and both of them wore an air of injured innocence, obviously expecting me to ask what was wrong. I turned to Jim instead.

"While you were away Marilyn began to extend her hours again. On the last afternoon she accused Tilly of doing a lousy job keeping the library organized, and Tilly told her she had no business being there in the afternoon at all," he said wearily. "They're still sulking."

I wanted to walk out. "What a pair of bloody-minded cows. I'm sorry you were stuck with this."

"It wasn't pleasant. I'm glad you're back." Jim hadn't smiled once that morning. I felt guilty. I'd left him holding far too much.

Marilyn chose that moment to come into the workroom. "How was your Whistler trip?" She darted a sideways look at me.

"Fine, thanks."

"Did you stay at Whistler or did you ski Blackcomb too?"

"I – er – we went to Blackcomb, yes."

"They have that new high speed lift, Excelerator, don't they? Did you use it?"

"Yes. Have you been there, Marilyn?"

"No. I just read up on it." She looked smug.

"Why?"

"I was interested." The tone was casual but her black eyes were avid.

I walked out of the workroom and over to the desk in the middle of the library. Marilyn had looked up the place I'd been on holiday. I felt my jaw muscles tighten, and a warning pulse beat behind my right eye. A migraine coming.

Al and I patched up our relationship, and he joined me at Easter. We went to Mt. Tremblant in Quebec for a snowy, sensual four day weekend. The night after he'd gone home, I was enjoying being alone again, when he phoned.

"What's the name of that weird woman you got volunteering in the library?"

"Marilyn. Why do you ..."

"You got a problem, honey. While I've been up in Quebec with you, she's been phoning my work, trying to get information about me, about the college, everything. My boss hauled me up first thing this morning. Said some dame from Toronto told him she's my girlfriend, she met me skiing in Quebec at Christmas and she wants my phone numbers, at work and at home, 'cause she's coming down to surprise me. Christ!"

My hand on the receiver had gone white.

"She left her name and address so he could send material on the college. That's how I know it's her. Dundas Street, right?"

"Yes. Al ..."

"You gotta get rid of this one, honey."

"She's as good as gone."

After a night spent seething with rage, I went into work and told Jim.

"How do you think she found his work-place?"

Jim pointed wordlessly at the blue coffee mug Al had given me, lying upside down on the drain board by the workroom sink. The name of the college was printed in tiny gold letters under the crest.

I phoned the social worker, told her Marilyn had to go.

"Marilyn is harmless, just pathetic," she said, when she heard what had happened. I didn't buy it. She agreed to come in to the school when I confronted Marilyn.

I saw the principal, told him Marilyn would be leaving and got him to agree that if she returned, she could be charged with trespassing. He looked at me oddly, but he didn't argue.

The social worker met me in the guidance department, semi-neutral territory on the ground floor, and Jim sent Marilyn downstairs to join us. The interview was brief. Marilyn began to scream at me as soon as I told her why she was finished.

"No, no you can't. You don't understand. You can't. I won't go."

I walked out and left the social worker to take her away. But I was shaking as I climbed the three flights of stairs back to the library.

"It's finished," I said to Jim as I poured coffee into the telltale blue and gold mug. "It's over."

"Good," he said.

"Oh yeah?" said Tilly.

Without Marilyn, work in the library increased but went better. All of us smiled more. Then at the beginning of May, the principal told me that Marilyn had phoned to say she'd been unfairly dismissed and wanted to return. I felt as if I'd been punched. When I could speak, my voice was a snarl.

"She wasn't unfairly dismissed, and she's never coming back. You do remember, don't you, that you agreed to charge her with trespassing if she reappeared?"

He looked at me. "Are you sure you're not over-reacting?"

"Positive."

Al broke up with me. He said he wanted someone who could commit. I was sad, but I was also relieved. No more pressure. I had enjoyed the sex and the attention but I just didn't want anything more. When I remembered the years I'd longed for Paul to commit to me, I felt guilty. Al deserved better.

For the third summer in a row I planned to return to the Findhorn Foundation. I signed up for a program called Life Purpose, but it was really just an excuse to be there. After the workshop I would visit my elderly cousins on the west coast of Scotland. I had started to pack a week before I was due to leave, when the phone rang. Marilyn. She sounded like a teenage tragedy queen.

"When you fired me, did you know I was in love with you?"

"No. And I don't care." I smashed the phone onto its base. I was still swearing when it rang again. I walked out of the house to escape, incoherent with rage.

For days the phone rang and rang and went on ringing. In turns I was polite but distant, rude, finally abusive but nothing worked. She pleaded, cried, carried on like a soap opera. Finally I listened to her. It was a last resort but it might make a difference. For an hour I held the phone at arm's length, while she raved. She loved my sensuality, she was jealous of the students I spent time with, she'd read what I read, researched where I went on holiday so some day we could talk about it, I'd looked at her and *made* her love me; I was her light, she was in shadow; I couldn't slam doors on her now that she'd discovered she was a lesbian. I had so much, she had so little, why was I so cruel? And on, and on. She'd attached my face to some fantasy of her own. The person she was describing didn't exist, as far as I could tell. It had nothing to do with me. The truth was I'd been bad-tempered and generally closed to her and everyone else at school, except for the students because they were my work.

"Look, Marilyn, life is hard," I said. "There is no relationship, and the job is finished. I'm hanging up now. Don't call again."

"What about forgiveness?" she wailed. I put the receiver down.

The phone stayed silent for the two remaining days. But I couldn't wait to get out of the country, to put an ocean between me and that bleating half-wit, to return to the place where people actually listened.

CHAPTER 17

Life Purpose

Scotland had never looked more beautiful. Cluny shone in the warm summer sunshine as I pulled my suitcase up the drive. I didn't have to be responsible, decisive, the boss. The phone wasn't going to ring for me. No one knew me; no one had expectations of me; I was anonymous; I could relax. I breathed in the clean air and felt my shoulders drop.

The Life Purpose workshop was supposed to help participants discover the essence of what touched them most and helped make life meaningful. "You will be guided towards an understanding of your current belief systems and the ways you relate to yourself and the world. You will appreciate the nature of your own, deeply personal, life-long journey towards fulfillment," the brochure had said. I'd paid little or no attention to the program description, and I moved blithely to Registration.

Late that evening I sat alone in the sun room, watching the sky darken. A large, pale moon was rising in the east. The afternoon had only been an introduction to the program, but I had felt overwhelmed and I didn't even know why. My eyes ached from crying. We had meditated on what brought us joy, what frustrated us, what we avoided. Everywhere I turned in my mind, I ran into my parents' injunction forbidding feelings. Grief, rage, love, loneliness swirled in me, picking up energy like a hurricane over water. We chose angels; mine was Courage. The card showed a little angel diving off a cliff. I wanted to groan. I couldn't measure up to that angel; I was the most risk-averse person I knew. Then the facilitators, Sue and Terry, asked us each to make a commitment for the week. Staring down at the little angel card, I committed to allowing myself to feel whatever came up for me.

"And to express those feelings?" asked Terry, as the group listened.

My stomach knotted up with fear. At that moment I was nothing but feeling. I was forty-five, and only Paul had ever appreciated the emotional side of me. This group of strangers was going to loathe me if my feelings spilled out of me like an overflowing bathtub for the whole week. I would loathe me. Even as I hesitated, tears began to run down my face and dampen the collar of my shirt. The group waited. Finally I nodded. My very bones felt like water.

If the first half day had been a marathon, how would I survive the rest of the week?

Life Purpose turned out to be a much more internal workshop than my other two had been, because, I suppose, our journeys were so personal. I was buffeted about by my emotions, but I didn't have to say much about them. When I did it was usually to only one person. One morning we did a series of meditations on ourselves as infants and young children. We were instructed to see ourselves as small perfect beings, before life began to mess us up. I couldn't. Under my closed lids, I remembered that I had been born with heart-lung problems that had required surgery when I was three. I had no memory of the operation, but I carried a long curving scar under my left breast from armpit to sternum. In the meditation I felt as if I'd been born flawed, and maimed further by Paul's death. As if I'd always needed defences. I wept through every meditation we did that morning.

I cried nearly every day that week, not necessarily because I was sad, more as a response, like ripples on water when a breeze blows. Anything would set me off. Other people's courage, or beauty or strength. I became a group joke. Not an unkind one, just someone whose tears provoked grins all around the circle. Even I laughed as I cried. It never occurred to me that I was making up for decades of emotional paralysis.

At the same time I revelled in all the beauty around me. The weather was glorious. The sun shone, the days were hot, the moon grew fuller every night. One afternoon we went out to the Findhorn River. We went our separate ways with instructions to find a solitary spot and sing. I squatted down on a rock by the peat brown water, glinting golden in the sunlight and sang every song I knew. I couldn't remember the last time I'd been so happy.

I did begin to understand that I felt trapped in my life in Toronto. I wasn't sure what needed to change or whether the trap was internal or external. I only knew that everyone there seemed to expect me to stay the same as I'd always been, while I felt profoundly altered since Paul's death.

"I'm not really so emotional," I said to one of the other guests. "I've just been a bit stuck since my husband died, well for the last six years. Normally I'm very logical and analytic. Pragmatic, even."

She looked as if she were trying not to laugh. "Are you sure you know what you're like? I'd have said you were very sensitive."

"No, not really. This is an aberration. At least, I think it is." *I hope it is. I don't want to be so sensitive. No, wait. I wasn't the one who told me to go to my room every time I was upset. My parents didn't want a sensitive child. My friends and family don't want ...* I was back to the split between Toronto expectations and Findhorn Foundation reality. I felt more confused than ever. What did I want? Who was I? Did I have a choice?

Late in the week we went to the ballroom for a session called Moving Out. There was an hour of body movement and then an extended guided meditation to music. I didn't recognize the piece but the melody seemed to drop me down into a place so far removed from the ballroom that I didn't hear half of the instructions. When I emerged, still entranced from the experience, I believed that my life's purpose was to celebrate God through dance.

The group began to share. I sat and listened, growing more and more confused. No one else had experienced anything like me. Eventually it was my turn.

"I didn't hear what you told us. I can't ... I don't ..." I shook my head to clear it. "Nothing makes sense. I saw myself as a dancer. Ballet. I was dancing my love for God. I was graceful, light but ... it's stupid. I was open for an answer, for something, but this isn't it. I don't love God; I can't dance. I got kicked out of ballet class when I was five and now I've got arthritis in my feet. I've never been graceful or light. How dumb can this get?" More tears. Why couldn't I stop falling apart?

They waited. When I'd calmed down, Sue said: "Maybe dancing is a metaphor. You don't have to understand everything all at once. Sit with it."

I nodded, wearily.

Late that night in the sanctuary as I brooded over the morning, a line from an old hymn slid into my mind. "Dance, dance, whoever you may be. / I am the Lord of the Dance, said he."

It's the dance of life, not a literal dance. I'm supposed to celebrate God as I move through my life. That's my life purpose. It made some kind of sense, but not much. Was I supposed to be a Christian? I couldn't imagine it. God always asked so much. I remembered the Bible stories of my childhood and shuddered. Fine for saints perhaps, but I was no saint and didn't want to be.

I was still thinking about this at tea break on Friday afternoon when the receptionist stopped me as I was heading out to the sunshine with my mug of Earl Grey.

"A woman phoned, asking for you. She didn't give her name. She wanted to know if you were here with your partner, Al Seti-something, when you were leaving and where you were going next. Well ..." he looked guilty. "I said you were here but not the guy and you were leaving tomorrow but I ... I began to realize that she ... wasn't quite ... look, I'm really sorry."

I sank down on a chair, my hand shaking so badly the tea spilled. Only Marilyn had bothered to learn Al's unusual last name. Only Marilyn didn't know we'd broken up in May. Only Marilyn would track me this far. She hadn't given up at all.

CHAPTER 18

Some Woman

My father met me at the airport. He took my suitcase and brushed a kiss against my cheek.

"Some woman's been calling, badgering me for your flight number. She wanted to meet you when you got in. I didn't tell her. She seemed a bit off."

We stopped at the place where I boarded my cat. The receptionist took my money, handed me the cat and said irritably, "Some woman's been calling here for days, wanting to know when you were expected back. She's completely mad."

The phone was silent when I walked into my house. But there was a message from my elderly Scottish cousin, her voice thin and distant. "Some woman called the day you left, wanting to know when you'd be home. She said she's a friend from work, but I thought she sounded very odd."

If I had any lingering impulse to celebrate God, it disappeared that day. A cloud of rage and fear swallowed me, cutting me off from the Foundation and from God. When the phone rang at nine the next morning, I stared at it but didn't pick up. Instead I went out to buy two phones with call display windows.

In the month that followed, the phone rang constantly but I never answered unless I recognized the number. There was no call display at work so I didn't answer the phone there at all. Deborah, the United Church minister who had conducted Paul's funeral, told me that Marilyn had been phoning the church office, trying to find out details about my wedding six and a half years ago. For a moment I pictured that ceremony, Paul and I with a Unitarian minister in front of the fire in the little stone-walled pub, family members seated at tables. Spring flowers on the tables and the bar. March sunlight lighting up the desk where we signed the marriage contract. Love, serenity and commitment. A long time ago. All gone now.

Obviously Marilyn had never learned that Paul was church-phobic. She refused to believe that no one at the United Church could tell her anything about my wedding. Eventually she located both Deborah and the retired minister who had buried my mother in 1978.

"I told her she had to leave you alone or she'd end up dead or in jail," Deborah said to me, "and she told me she didn't care, if you were with her."

I put my hand up to my pounding right temple.

"Doesn't that sound like a threat to you? I take it seriously. You have to call the police," Deborah said.

"I can't. What would I tell them, some maniac woman thinks she's in love with me and is making a lot of phone calls? They'd think I was nuts."

"You'd call fast enough if she was a man."

I was silent for a moment. I wanted to believe that this night-mare would disappear if I didn't react but it was getting harder and harder to ignore. "Okay, I'll call them."

Two uniformed cops, Doug and Kim, came to the library late one afternoon after Jim and Tilly had gone. I had dressed profes-sionally that day, worn make-up and dress pants with a jacket. Even polished my silver earrings. I was increasingly aware that I was fraying under the pressure, and I wanted to make sure the cracks didn't show. I greeted them with the detailed file I'd made on Marilyn.

The two listened carefully, examined my file and made a copy. Kim smiled reassuringly.

"Don't worry," she said. "We'll pay Marilyn a visit now and warn her off."

"Why not just be nice to her?" asked Jim the next day, when I told him about Kim and Doug. "That's all she wants."

"No. It isn't. I don't know what she wants, but it's like she's trying to devour me."

Doug called back later that day. Marilyn had refused point blank to stay away from me. Exasperated, they had taken her before a judge. The judge had no effect either. They brought in the social worker and a lawyer but the upshot was Marilyn spent the night in jail. Friday morning she was just as stubborn so the judge jailed her for the weekend.

I was relieved and appalled both. I would never look neurotic next to this kind of mad behaviour. On the other hand, what was it going to take to make her see sense?

She was released three days later after she finally caved in and signed a form promising to stay away from me. The phone calls began again.

I exercised, had regular therapy and massage sessions and stuck to a healthy diet. But I was clinging to sanity by my fingernails.

Doug and Kim told me to ask the neighbours whether Marilyn had been seen in the vicinity. So I took a picture of her across the road to Lawrence, who sat on his porch drinking coffee seven days a week. Lawrence knew everything that happened on the street.

"Yeah, I know her," he said, barely glancing at the photo. "She's around most nights. She's looking for a house in the neighbourhood, asked me how much I thought yours was worth."

"What?" I whispered. "Are you sure?"

"Sure." He tossed the dregs from his coffee cup off the side of the porch.

From then on, I looked every night and I saw her often, talking to Lawrence, or skulking in the lane that separated the back of my house from the park. When I didn't see her I thought I could see her shadow. I never confronted her, partly because I felt she longed for that and partly because I was afraid I'd hit her. Paul had built this house to let in maximum light. To prevent someone seeing inside, I had to keep the blinds pulled. The house was in perpetual gloom. I was in hell.

I told the police she was appearing on my street, and they came by occasionally but their visits never coincided with hers. I didn't want to seem neurotic so I didn't call again. My migraines returned, stronger and more frequent.

"How long is this going to go on?" I raged to my therapist.

"Um, well, the bad news is that obsessive people don't hear 'no' and usually persist until their obsession shifts to someone else. It can take years."

"What's the good news?"

There wasn't any.

Only at work did I feel safe. The library was on the third floor of the school, I was there from 8 a.m. to well after 4 p.m. and Marilyn could not reach me. It was different everywhere else.

I changed my home phone number to an unlisted one. The next day she called the library repeatedly. "Where is she? What's her new number?"

"I'm not telling you. Stop calling," said Jim.

"Give it up, Marilyn, she's never going to see you," said Tilly.

"I just need to know where she is, what she's doing and who she's with, and then I'll be all right," Marilyn sobbed.

I wanted to kill her. Every time a really tough student came into the library, I had to bite my tongue to keep from offering him cash to beat Marilyn to a pulp.

She showed up on my route to school, standing next to a traffic light, only a foot or so away from the car, her eyes glued onto me. I felt unclean. The light was red. I wanted to jerk the steering wheel, drive straight into her, mash her body into the light pole, feel the splat of flesh and the crunch of bone. I gripped the wheel white-knuckled, and stayed in my lane as the light turned green and I eased forward.

That night, after I'd hidden the car in the garage, shut every blind and turned off every light, I sat in the upstairs guest room. The only window stared into the blank wall of the house next door. I lit one small lamp and huddled on the couch.

Anger and violence. When someone else held all the power,

anger was too risky. It made me vulnerable. Safety lay in repression, in self-control.

Twenty years earlier I'd been engaged to Nevil. He was fourteen years older than me, divorced, good-looking, charming, with beautiful manners. He'd bought a house in Aurora, north of Toronto, and I'd moved in with him. I thought I was in love, but I worried about his mood swings - one minute depression and the next anger. Once I tried to walk away from him during an argument, and he clipped me on the jaw. There was no visible mark, and he acted as if nothing had happened. I might have wondered whether I'd imagined it except that my neck and jaw muscles ached for two days. After that I asked a guidance counsellor at my school for advice. She sent me to a middle-aged woman psychiatrist. I'd never been to one before. There was no couch in her office, only a comfortable chair. I took a deep breath.

"I'm supposed to marry this man in eight months, but I'm having doubts. He has spells of depression, and I don't know how to help him. And sometimes he picks these fights for no reason. If it happens at bedtime he goes to sleep and I lie awake. I can't afford sleepless nights. I get horrible head colds as soon as I miss some sleep. I've even had pneumonia a couple of times. My family isn't emotional; I've never experienced all this – this turmoil before, and I don't know if I can handle it."

She considered me. "What do you do with your anger?"

I stared at her. "I told you, I grew up in an unemotional family. I don't get angry."

"Everybody gets angry. All you've said is that no one expressed anger, but everyone feels it. You teach, you teach teenagers. You must get angry."

I smiled. "Oh, well, I get irritated, certainly. Then I get tired. You can't lose your temper with students. As soon as that happens, they've won. But really angry? No."

"What about when you were a child?"

I'd actually been angry often as a child at my younger brother. My mother had said to me, very quietly, "You must control your temper. I used to get angry too until someone told me to count to ten before I spoke and swallow hard. I learned; so can you."

She must have been right. I never heard her angry aside from the occasional pot slammed in the kitchen, and I learned to stay out of the kitchen then. I practised counting and swallowing anger. I wasn't always successful, but I hid any failures from my mother and substituted snide comments and sarcasm for anger. My brother was less verbal than I was, and two years younger. One day he swung a fist at me in response. Somehow he got me squarely in the solar plexus. I doubled over, unable to breathe, making terrifying sucking noises. In that moment the balance of power shifted. I never baited him again, and he never hit me.

"I learned not to be angry early on."

She shook her head in disbelief, and I began to feel annoyed. This was pointless.

"Do you not think there might be some connection between your suppressed anger and the head colds you say you keep getting?"

I opened my mouth but no words came.

"Perhaps you could experiment a little. Try expressing your irritation more. See if it makes a difference."

Silence. I dropped my gaze before the compassion in her eyes.

"Is it safe to be angry with Nevil?"

I shook my head.

I didn't see her again.

Three months before the wedding day Nevil lost his temper because I'd worn a push-up bra to a medical appointment with a male doctor. It was so ludicrous I laughed. He knocked me down.

The next day I waited until he had gone out before I phoned my mother to ask if I could come home, with the cat. I never said why.

Marilyn's relentless stalking was threatening my lifetime pattern of self-control. I was powerless to stop her and more terrified than ever because this time, the rage, the murderous violence was mine, and held back only by a thread.

I changed my route to work. It took me ten minutes longer to get to school, but at least I didn't see her and therefore I couldn't run her down.

A week later I glanced out of the library window as I picked books up from a table and she was there, standing in the parking lot beside my car, staring at it as if she thought it would tell her the way I'd come to school. She was there three days running. I called the police again. This time they caught her. Jim and I watched from the library window as she was escorted into the unmarked car and driven off. She spent two weeks in jail that time.

When she came out, she managed to find my unlisted phone number and the calls began again.

The Foundation seemed far away. I thought of it when my therapist suggested that I smudge the library with sage to clear Marilyn's energy. But the woman who had pictured celebrating God through dance had been erased.

I skied every weekend, but my heart sank each time I turned the car back toward the city, knowing Marilyn lurked there, waiting for me.

No one could help. Few people phoned except Marilyn; they didn't have my number. My world was shrinking into a circle that included only Marilyn and me.

My father wanted me to move into a high rise apartment with a security guard.

"Dad, she found out my unlisted phone number within a month. A security guard isn't going to stop her. And why should I change my whole life because of one demented woman?"

I was feeling increasingly demented myself. My only hope was the upcoming year off. I planned to spend the first three months in the Foundation and hoped it wasn't too late to find the best part of me again.

Her trial was scheduled late in July.

Al hadn't called since our break up fourteen months earlier. My father went on holiday with his wife. I felt abandoned. But Kathleen gave me a lift to court, fearing I might not be able to drive safely between anxiety and rage. Five friends, including the minister, came to the court for moral support. Lawrence was there, looking around for the coffee machine. The courthouse building was crowded and noisy, a warren of cramped hallways and small rooms. We were frisked when we entered. I pressed my lips together tightly to stop them trembling. I wore a white top and skirt, thinking of the good guy in cowboy movies, and deeply aware I'd wanted to murder Marilyn for almost a year. I was terrified at the prospect of testifying, in case the hatred and evil inside me spewed out like toxic waste.

Leaving my friends at the courtroom door, I went in search of the crown lawyer. He was young and thin, working in a small, windowless, paper-strewn office. He had the file on Marilyn open on the desk, and the two cops were in there with him. There was hardly room for me.

"Marilyn can answer two questions all right but by the third she explodes like rotten fruit," Doug said. I felt queasy. The phone rang. I jumped.

The lawyer listened and answered in monosyllables. When he hung up he was smiling.

"Good news, I think. Marilyn has agreed to plead guilty if she can see you first to apologize."

"*What?* No. She doesn't want to apologize, she wants my attention. It's just another ploy."

"I know." His smile vanished. "But we need her to plead guilty. We have a very thin case because she's never identified herself on the phone. The only witness besides you is Lawrence, and he can only say she's in the neighbourhood a lot."

I bit my lip, raised my clenched fists to my chest. No one could control her. Even here, in the heart of the legal system, she was manipulating everyone.

"Doug and Kim will be with you. Think what it will be like if she gets off," added the lawyer.

Twenty minutes later I stood in a crowded hallway, my hands still clenched, surrounded by my friends and the two cops. Marilyn was flanked by her lawyer and her social worker. She fixed me with her black eyes, just as if we were alone, gave a brief "apology" in case she'd "upset" my elderly father and launched into a rant. I'd been unfair, this was all my fault, she'd tried to do a good job, I'd betrayed her. I stood in silence, my chest tight, my breathing laboured, determined not to speak. On and on Marilyn raged. Fifteen minutes later, Kim cut in.

"Enough. We need to go into the courtroom."

"Will you shake hands?" asked Marilyn, as if she hadn't been raining abuse and accusation on me.

"No."

She pleaded guilty and got a two year suspended sentence. It was fair enough, but it didn't guarantee any change. Judges had told her to stay away from me before this. If I hadn't had a year off work lined up, I would have quit, just to get away.

The last I saw of her, Marilyn was standing on the courthouse steps, staring after Kathleen's car as if she was trying to memorize the licence plate. My hands shook.

"Drive, drive," I muttered to Kathleen.

So, seven years after Paul's death, my life in Toronto collapsed. Logic, hard work, reason, even the legal system had failed me and I'd ended up trapped in a closed and dangerous circle. The only way out was to cut and run.

CHAPTER 19

Escape

I didn't relax until the plane had lifted off the ground and headed northeast toward Glasgow, Scotland. Then I let my head fall back and closed my eyes. No more phone calls, no more peering out from behind blinds at shadows, no more driving to work with my attention on the sidewalk rather than the traffic. All that was over. I almost smiled.

But who was I? I wanted to revert to the person I'd been during Life Purpose, a woman who was open and light-filled. Eliminate the dark, demonic presence I'd been the past two years. Was it possible? For seven years I'd been unrecognizable in my own eyes. First paralyzed by grief, then poisoned by rage. The Foundation would cope with grief, but I couldn't see people accepting rage. Could I really find the sanity and goodness that had once been uppermost in me in the Findhorn Foundation?

Yes. I straightened up in my seat. Away from Marilyn, I'd be normal. Maybe I'd even be enlightened after three months. I'd left Paul's picture behind in Canada along with my grief. This was a new start. Smiling, I waved aside the steward's offer of soft drinks and requested a gin and tonic.

I should have remembered my cousin Kate's words from four years ago: "You can't run away here. Your issues surface, whatever they are, and you have to confront them."

A few weeks later on a rainy Monday morning I looked incredulously into Sigrid's furious face. I had just asked her if she'd help me with my breakfast shift in the dining room the next day. I had worked with her on her Friday breakfast shift; it seemed like a fair exchange. We stood beside the serving table in the dining room of Cluny Hill College while people eddied around us, getting food, or taking their dirty dishes into the stillroom to be washed, and she hissed at me like a feral cat.

"Breakfast shift? No. I tell ... I say ... I not work with you again. Never."

I stared at her. Most of the time Sigrid's heavy German accent and convoluted constructions made her speech nearly incomprehensible. The only time I could understand her easily was when she was criticizing me, which was happening more and more. Then she used simple words and short sentences.

"What? Why not?"

"You cut my power." She sawed the air so furiously with her hand that someone reaching for the milk had to duck. "I never work with you again. Change schedule."

"But ... why?"

"You! You are big problem. You need many more months than three to fix you. They all see." She stormed off. A couple of guests avoided my eyes as they followed her to the exit. Humiliation and bewilderment churned in my stomach. No one, not even people who disliked me, had ever told me I was impossible to work with. My face burned.

I had been trying to cope with Sigrid for a month, ever since joining the Living in Community as a Guest (LCG) program. I had hoped this extended stay in the Foundation would enable me to embody the lessons I'd learned in the three workshops I'd taken, lessons that had dissolved each time I returned to Toronto. But this morning the Foundation was feeling much more like Toronto than the peaceful haven I'd imagined.

Like me, Sigrid was an LCG who worked in the dining room. She was slight, blonde, German and ten years older than me. She'd been here one week longer than I had, which she seemed to think gave her a huge advantage. All our communication was one-way. I struggled so much to understand her that I never got to express myself. I suppose Sigrid was as frustrated by my failure as I was. I was trying really hard to prove to myself that I was the co-operative, reasonable, hard-working, *good* person I'd once taken for granted, and obviously failing. Sigrid – well, I didn't know what Sigrid was trying to prove. I never understood what made her lash out at me. I felt too shamed and too confused to talk to anyone else in the Foundation about this, but whenever I saw her glaring at me from the middle of a group, I was sure she was criticizing me. I began to withdraw.

Fortunately I had found a therapist by this time, a woman named Elke, a former Foundation member now living in the wider community.

"Sigrid is completely irrational," I said. "Work is work. Why does she have to drag all this melodrama into it?"

Elke raised her eyebrows but didn't speak.

"I work hard to get it done as well and efficiently as possible. Working in the dining room is not like teaching, aside from working with the guests, I mean, showing them what work here in the Foundation is like. It's – well - mechanical. You know what the tasks are: the dish washing, the vacuuming, the teas, the clean plates and cutlery for the next meal, all that. It's completely straightforward and doesn't require a lot of thought. You just do it."

I couldn't read Elke's expression. But what I was saying was so obvious that she must agree. I rubbed my forehead wearily.

"There was this woman, in Toronto ..." I told her about Marilyn, although I was careful to downplay my extreme reaction to her. It was the first time I'd mentioned Marilyn here.

"And Sigrid reminds me of Marilyn," I finished. "Maybe it's because she's so irrational."

"Or is it that you don't cope well with an emotional approach?" said Elke. "You want everything to make sense, to be cut and dried. People aren't always like that. Work, too, is a part of everything else, not a separate world."

"But ..."

"We all have parts in us that aren't particularly rational. My guess is that if you refuse to acknowledge that you too can be emotional and irrational, you'll keep meeting people like Marilyn and Sigrid."

"*What?*" I recoiled. I was here to leave Marilyn behind. I couldn't meet more people like her. Surely Sigrid was an anomaly.

"The parts of ourselves that we refuse to accept show up in the people around us. If you reject and repress your feelings, inevitably the people around you are going to seem more and more emotional, just to balance you out."

"What a hideous and revolting thought." I could remember my emotional and irrational side very clearly, though I didn't say so. I just chose to reject it, the way I thought everyone should.

Elke shrugged. I felt almost too weak to stand at the end of the session.

Sigrid demanded a conflict facilitation session with Ulrike, a Foundation member who spoke German as well as English fluently. It took two weeks to set up because Ulrike was on holiday. During the waiting period I woke up every morning with a headache.

This was a spiritual community and I already felt guilty because I wasn't a spiritual person. If I couldn't work well, I wouldn't have a place here at all. If I couldn't stay in Toronto and I didn't fit in here, where would I go?

Thanks to the therapy sessions my shame and humiliation had given way to anger by the time we reached the meeting, but my stomach was churning. I imagined the two of us would have to end up locked into loving agreement, and I knew bloody well Sigrid wasn't going to give way. That left me. But pretend to be meek, lie down for this raging woman I couldn't even understand? Unthinkable.

Ulrike invoked clarity and understanding. Her manner was serene. Her English was excellent with only a soft blur to suggest it wasn't her native language. She looked at us both, then began to speak, first in English, then in German.

"The purpose of this meeting, which you requested, Sigrid, is to open communication between the two of you so that you can understand what has been going wrong. Perhaps you can clear away some of the problem you've been having, perhaps not."

No enforced forgiveness, then. I blinked with relief.

"Who would like to begin?" There was a pause. Ulrike looked at me. I shook my head. Sigrid's lip curled and she burst into a torrent of German. Ulrike listened intently.

"Sigrid says that during a Friday afternoon shift she was leading, you took over and insisted on running the shift yourself and dismissing the guests."

That was the cause of this whole crisis? Between relief and exasperation, I felt dizzy.

"Friday afternoon, three weeks ago?"

Sigrid nodded.

"That's not what - oh for God's sake. Yes, Sigrid was leading the shift, with me and two guests." I spoke to Ulrike; I was fed up with Sigrid. "We'd cleaned up from lunch and re-organized all the tables and chairs for the Friday night celebration dinner, you know, so all the workshop groups could sit together. We were doing fine in terms of time until Sigrid decided she wanted it all re-arranged again, in a different way. The guests set the tables as she said she wanted, but then she changed her mind and wanted that all done again too. It was nearly the end of their last shift and I could see they wanted to go off and get ready for dinner. I protested, because I didn't think changing one hundred and forty place settings was worth the work, but Sigrid said she was an artist and beauty mattered. So I suggested she let the guests go and I could stay late and reset the tables."

Ulrike translated this. Sigrid burst into speech again but Ulrike touched her arm and she fell silent.

"Sigrid didn't want that, but the guests looked ready to mutiny. I got the basket of blessing cards we hand out at the end of the week and offered it to her. She walked away and disappeared into the stillroom. So I tuned out the guests, reset the tables and asked her if she wanted to check them. She wouldn't speak to me, and I left. I had no idea she'd still be angry on Monday, let alone insist on this meeting, three weeks later."

Sigrid glared at me. I tried to keep my expression impassive.

"I suppose she is technically right, I did take over when she refused to listen to my suggestion, but I thought then and I still think now it was a good compromise. She got her 'artistic' vision," I tried hard to keep the sarcasm out of my voice, "I worked late to help her achieve it, and the guests weren't penalized."

Ulrike translated. I turned to look directly at Sigrid at last.

"I'm fine to have you in charge of the shift, Sigrid, and I'm ready to help you achieve whatever it is you want, but you can't expect me to sit there in silence while you try to make guests work longer than they should because you can't make up your mind what you want."

Sigrid responded vehemently and at length. But all Ulrike said was: "Sigrid feels you do not listen to her feedback and do not respect her."

"Sigrid never does anything but give me feedback, all negative, as if I'm some kind of delinquent teenager, and I can never respond because she says I don't understand, so yes, I tune out."

Another passionate outburst in German. Sigrid hadn't waited for translation. Ulrike interrupted, speaking calmly. Sigrid's face turned blank. She went silent. Ulrike said in English, "I am telling Sigrid that feedback must be invited before it is given. This is a rule that she has not heard, apparently."

I hadn't heard it either, as a matter of fact, but I liked the sound of it. Sigrid looked indignant. Neither of us spoke.

"Is there anything you wish to say to Sigrid now that you know what the problem has been?" Ulrike added.

I drew a deep breath. Unclenched my hands. Whether I stayed in the Foundation or left it, I wasn't backing down after all this.

"I'm sorry you were upset, Sigrid." I looked directly at her. "But I haven't come here to be silent just because you may not like what I say."

Sigrid looked nonplussed. I couldn't tell what she was thinking.

"You do not change?" she muttered. I shook my head.

Ulrike glanced at us both. Her thoughts weren't obvious either.

"I think we will end here," she said. "Perhaps you will both meditate on this and discuss it if necessary in your next department meeting. In the meantime, I would like to invoke patience and understanding in the Dining Room Department."

By the time I'd climbed the stairs to the sanctuary, all my defiance had drained away and I was trembling. I pulled a blanket around me and sank onto a cushion. At least there would be neither demands nor feedback here. I had hoped to find safety and a new beginning in the Findhorn Foundation but I felt more battered than anything else. My vision of myself as open, light-filled and loving was dead in the water.

CHAPTER 20
The Mystery School

"At least I got equal time, for once," I said to Elke in my next therapy session. "That was good. I was heard, and I finally understood what Sigrid was on about. I was irritated but not foaming at the mouth the way I was with Marilyn. But – I don't know how spiritual I was. I was pretty pissed off."

Elke frowned. "You have an odd idea of what is spiritual. You said to Sigrid what you needed to say. You stayed centred but you didn't attack her. That's good. It's adult. Stop worrying about spirituality."

Despite Elke's comment I had a clear picture of a spiritual person. Enlightened people didn't get angry, didn't lose control. They always seemed to know what was right for them; they had a lot of confidence. They forgave other people. They also had a clear, two-way line of communication with God. That wasn't me.

I believed in God, and I often thought I was right. Nothing else was true. I spent time in the sanctuary, but that was mostly because no one would interrupt me there. I occasionally told God what I thought of Him, but I didn't have the patience to stay awake while waiting for an answer. Hardly spiritual.

"The Findhorn Foundation is a Mystery School."
The skin on the back of my neck prickled.
"Mystery Schools are places where neophytes and initiates on the spiritual path undergo the tests and training of a higher consciousness. The Foundation is a Mystery School without a guru. Our belief is that God is within everyone, in all the people we meet

here. No matter how irritating or annoying they seem." Eric, a senior Foundation member, smiled at the incredulous looks from the group. "We are teachers for each other. It's why we need to appreciate, even love, all the people we meet."

It was another LCG Thursday afternoon education session. The idea of a Mystery School caught my attention immediately. Learning and teaching each other appealed much more to me than unconditional love.

"When we come to the Foundation, we enter a transition state, we let go of our previous patterns. Sometimes this feels like a series of crises, painful moments and periods of confusion. Often this transition discourages people, and they leave. But those who are willing to move forward merge with a deeper, divine identity and become people with more light and love in them. Peter Caddy, one of the founders of the Findhorn Foundation, described this place as a 'graveyard for egos.'" Eric paused. "Of course, not everyone is willing to move forward, even people who stay on longer. For those people, life in the Foundation is a continuing struggle. But we all have difficulty at times."

I had stopped breathing. "Crises, pain and periods of confusion" described my life since Paul's death. I let out a huge breath and felt tearful. I was not a misfit. This was normal.

I hadn't felt normal in seven years.

Afterward I stood alone under the beech tree at the top of the garden. I had always loved being a student, and the idea of a Mystery School hooked me. For the first time I wondered what it might be like to live in the Foundation long term.

We had monthly interviews with the LCG focalizer and in October she asked me how long I was planning to stay. I had no answer. Should I leave in November and get on with the rest of my plans for the year off? Should I stay for Christmas? Finally I decided to follow the example of Eileen Caddy and ask for guidance in meditation. I didn't really expect anything to happen but I held the question -*when should I leave*- in my mind as I sat in the sanctuary after dinner that night. Slowly a message took shape in words in my mind: *Do not return to teaching.*

I opened my eyes. This was ridiculous. Teaching was who I was, how I earned money. I shook my head and waited for this "answer" to clear, but nothing changed. After ten minutes or so, I tiptoed away from the sanctuary, hoping God wouldn't notice. That night I consulted my friend Noreen, an Irish nun on leave from her order.

"Pay attention to your dreams," she said in her musical County Cork accent. "And ask again." So I did. The dream came the next night.

I am standing in an airport with a crowd of people, all waiting for the same flight. When the attendants open the gates everyone surges forward, carrying me with them. The sign says Las Vegas. I'm paying money to go to Las Vegas? This is a mistake. I hated it when I was there with Paul. I want out. But – my luggage is on the plane, and I'm being pushed toward the ramp. No. I'm not going to Las Vegas. I turn and begin to struggle back against the current of people.

I mulled this dream over for a day, but the meaning seemed clear. Returning to Toronto was a gamble. A pay-cheque and other people's expectations weren't enough to pull me back. I hadn't enjoyed life there since Paul died. Marilyn had driven me out and I was happy to be out. However bizarre it would sound to my father and my colleagues, I wanted to explore the Mystery School of the Findhorn Foundation. I wanted to be a person with more light and love in me.

I requested an interview for the next Foundation Year Program (FYP), scheduled to begin in March.

The interview was conducted by a three person team, Judith from the Education Department, the same serene and smiling Judith who had guided my Game of Transformation in 1994, Rory, an Irish-American man who had focalized the last FYP group and Gill from Spiritual and Personal Development, the Foundation version of a Human Resources department. They asked a few practical questions about money and my responsibilities in Canada. I thought again about my father, brother and sister, preoccupied with spouses, children and work. I thought about teaching, the endless demands, my exhaustion. I thought about Marilyn.

"Absolutely nothing is holding me back."

Gill led a meditation so we could attune to my request. We sat quietly for a few minutes, and I tried to empty my mind. Then she invoked the Angel of the Findhorn Foundation.

"Imagine the energy of the Findhorn Foundation as a column of light. I invite you, Leslie, to see yourself step into the column of light. Just notice what happens."

There was silence. I felt too shy to barge into the column of light in my meditation, so I looked down and silently asked if I was worthy. The light moved around me. Tears filled my eyes. When I looked up the light felt like a benediction.

Afterwards Gill invited me to share what had happened.

"I ... er ... I felt sure that I was in the right place, when I was standing in the light," I said. Hardly a detailed description, but I didn't want them to see me as someone who ignored instructions. After a moment, Gill turned to the others.

"I got a yes," said Rory.

Judith looked at me quizzically. "I saw you step into the column. Then the light became a whirlwind, and you disappeared. I was just starting to get worried about you when the light cleared and you were lying on a bench, wearing sunglasses and looking relaxed." She chuckled. "I think that's a yes."

Gill considered me. "I saw you in the light. It seemed to go into and through you so your whole body was light except for a dark area in your spine, like a piece of turtle shell. I imagine this is your resistance. If you deal with your own resistance, then yes."

This wasn't entirely reassuring, but overcoming resistance was just an act of will. I was convinced I was meant to be there. Pushing aside images of whirlwinds and dark areas in my spine, I said yes. The others nodded. I was in.

That night at dinner I celebrated my acceptance with LCG friends. But the next day during my morning work shift I began to feel queasy. By noon I had a searing headache with alternate hot and cold sweats.

For the next few hours I sat in a chair beside the sink in my room, waiting to throw up. I had a cold cloth on my hot neck and woolly socks on my freezing feet. Some time around 4 p.m., I realized that I was terrified. What kind of change was waiting for me on the one-year program? Who would I be at the end of it? Eric had called the Foundation a "graveyard for the ego;" would the people who knew me in Canada still like me when I'd finished? I put my burning forehead against the cool porcelain of the sink. My stomach steadied a bit, and my hot and cold sweats began to subside. But I still missed dinner and the LCG meeting that night.

In Canada, all obstacles fell smoothly away. I extended my leave from teaching for another year, sold my house, put my belongings into storage and returned to Great Britain on the 28th of February 1997, ready to begin the Foundation Year Program.

The first of March was cold, clear and sparkling.

CHAPTER 21

Psychosynthesis Essentials

"So you'll be staying on for a second year then?" Stewart said, as he poured a can of lager into two glasses. We'd finished a kitchen clean-up shift, and were sitting on the bed in his room, our backs against the wall.

"Och, aye." I grinned. I didn't sound like him, but I enjoyed trying. I loved the Glaswegian accent.

"How was your week in Toronto?"

"Efficient. I resigned from work, made my one year leave of absence permanent. My family wasn't too impressed, but they didn't say much." Actually I think they'd been stunned silent. But education in Ontario was under attack from the government at the time, the budget had been slashed and a lot of people were leaving.

Stewart nodded. He'd done the same thing before coming to the Foundation, quit his Administrative job in a high school in Glasgow. His wife still hadn't forgiven him.

"Are you taking any time off in March? It's your year end."

"No away time. I've signed up for the Psychosynthesis Essentials Workshop."

"Sounds more like work than a holiday to me." He lifted his glass to toast me. "Cheers. Here's to your second year."

Stewart had started his Foundation Year Program six months after me, in the September 1997 group. I'd only really got to know him at Christmas, when I'd come back to Cluny one afternoon after a snowy walk up from Forres and found him hemming his jeans in front of the fire in the lounge. Large stitches in white thread showed up clearly against blue denim. I watched with a grin as three different women offered to hem the jeans for him. He refused politely each time. Eventually he looked over at me.

"Does no one believe a man can hem his own trousers? You'd never know this place was a hotbed of feminism."

"Perhaps they just want to see the job well done."

"Are you going to offer too?"

"No. I'd be worse than you, even."

"Mocked in me own home," he said ruefully. "Do you want to have dinner in the dining room with me tonight?"

We became best friends that night over steamed vegetables and baked potatoes with cheese sauce. Stewart worked in Cluny kitchen. His cooking and his sense of humour won me over completely. I'd been strongly tempted right then to take the relationship further, but I'd had a brief and disastrous foray into a relationship with a long-term Cluny member in my first month and it had made me cautious. It was just as well. Stewart reconciled with his wife over Christmas. They continued to live separately, he in the Foundation, she in Glasgow, but he went "down the road" every six or seven weeks to see her. Even so, he didn't feel any need to be faithful to her. His company lit up my days in the Foundation but I opted for shared dinners, beers, late night conversations and celibacy.

Psychosynthesis Essentials was a one week workshop based on work by Roberto Assagioli, who says that the individual needs to integrate all the parts of herself into a synthesis, in order to form a more cohesive self. Exactly what I had known I needed, ever since a mask-making session at the start of my student year.

In the first week as full time students of the Foundation, we had meditated and then created three masks, one of our past selves, one of our present selves and one for the selves we imagined we'd be in the future. My mask of the past showed a young, smiling face with frightened eyes and a wrinkled forehead. The mouth was closed. I wanted to cry when I looked at it. The mask for the present was divided vertically. One side was in black and white, with an unsmiling mouth and a blank stare. The other side was jagged, in fiery colours of red, orange and yellow, the mouth open in a scream. The hair stood straight up and eye was wild. This mask looked utterly demented. I did begin to cry then. The last one, the mask for the future, had a mouth open as if speaking, wide eyes and a rainbow. The face of someone at peace. I hoped it would be prophetic, but after a year that resembled Judith's vision of a whirlwind, lesson after difficult lesson, I knew I wasn't anywhere near the serenity of the third mask.

On the first morning of the Psychosynthesis workshop, Frances, the facilitator, invited us into a meditation. She told us to imagine a bus driving across a field and stopping beside us. Even after a year in the Foundation I wasn't particularly disciplined at meditation. I often grew sleepy or drifted into daydreams. But this time a picture rolled out in my head as clearly as a film.

"There are people on the bus," she said. "When the door opens, look and see first who the driver is."

As a yellow school bus rumbled over a stubble field in my meditation I dutifully "looked" without any particular expectation. When I saw my father at the wheel, my jaw dropped. I barely heard the next instruction.

"Notice the first person who gets off the bus and ask that person some questions."

Still completely bemused, I saw a woman I didn't recognize step down from the bus, dressed beautifully but incongruously in a red "power" suit and carrying a brief case. She was dark haired and decisive in manner. I cleared my throat, but before I could speak she said abruptly: "I'm on holiday. I'm not hanging around here."

"Wait a minute. I'm supposed to interview you."

"That's your problem." Turning on her high heel she strode off across the field as smoothly as if it had been a hardwood floor. I stared after her. A little girl sidled off the bus next and looked anxiously up at me. Ignoring her, I called after the red-suited woman, but she never looked back.

"The driver of the bus is the main influence in your life. The first person off the bus is your major subpersonality, your own sense of yourself," said Frances when the meditation was over. "The next person is an aspect of you that is important but not as familiar."

I sat rigid with horror. My father was still at the wheel of my life? *My father?* And the "major subpersonality," that confident, powerful woman in a red suit, was my version of myself? Something was wrong. But more to the point, she'd just walked out. Without her I felt dislocated, abandoned and afraid. As for the little girl, I didn't want to know her. But I did know her; she was hugely emotional, needy, demanding, lost ... I couldn't stand her. I felt panicky.

"We are all made up of many subpersonalities. Usually there is a dominant one, with which we are familiar, but there are many others that we don't know as well, perhaps aren't aware of at all. In Psychosynthesis we try to get to know them so integration becomes easier."

I closed my eyes to blot Frances out and hold myself together. It felt as if I might shatter.

For the whole week of the workshop I had vertigo. I was slightly nauseous and tearful too, as if I had been betrayed and ambushed. But I said nothing. Even without my red-suited, logical subpersonality, I knew it was no one's fault. I had asked for this.

Of course it explains a lot, I said to myself. That red-suited woman is my attempt to live up to Dad's ideal, which I can't believe I'm still clinging to, even here in the Foundation. She is the one he approves of. I thought she was me; well, I guess she's the one I want people to see, but she's not the only one, that's all. It's no big deal. I wanted to know all this, right?

But I shuddered and felt ill. What good did knowing do when I hated what else I saw, the parts that were not Dad's creation? I knew that red-suited woman, I liked her, she was acceptable, useful, familiar. Only ... she was gone. In fact ... hadn't she'd stepped down from Commander-in-Chief several years ago, when Paul had died? She couldn't bear all that sloppy grief. And surely she hadn't been front and centre while I was living with Paul. The subpersonality that lived with Paul was warm, loving and filled with laughter. I had assumed that she had died with him, but now I wondered if she was the one who couldn't stop grieving. So was the Red-Suited Woman older, if she predated Paul and the period after his death?

Yes, older, especially if she's the one created for Dad. I guess she's come back to take charge again since Paul died. She's been trying to propel me past all the grieving. Except it hasn't worked very well. No wonder she's fed up and walking out.

How many people was I? I remembered thinking that Foundation members were mad during my Experience Week. I understood it now; I felt as mad as any of them.

I must have been mad before I came here, mad since Paul's death, I thought. I just didn't realize it. The Foundation uncovers madness, it doesn't create it. Is that better or worse?

I had no idea.

I might not have been able to stand that little girl part of me, but I couldn't escape her. In another meditation a day later I relived my "earliest memory," a memory that felt completely new to me. I was a young child, perhaps three, and I'd just had heart surgery to correct a congenital problem. I woke up in a hospital bed with my mother in a nearby chair. I was so happy to see her after being alone and terrified that I could hardly bear it. She kissed me very carefully and held my hand.

"Shh, shh, it's all right. You're doing well. The doctor is happy with you. Look at this lovely book I've brought you." The book had a bright yellow cover, and pictures, but I wasn't interested. I gripped her fingers frantically.

"We'll read the book, and I'll stay until you're asleep but then I have to leave. I'm staying with Granny so I'll come back tomorrow."

"No ... Mummy ... don't go ..." I could only croak. My throat was too sore to speak. But I saw immediately in her tense expression and averted eyes that she was horribly upset. I was so frightened I went silent. What if she did not come back? With a huge effort I swallowed my anguish. If I stayed awake, she'd *have* to stay with me. I pretended to admire the new book. My self-control reassured her, and she turned back to show me the pictures. But no matter how hard I struggled, darkness overwhelmed me. The next time I woke I was alone.

I managed to choke this story out in the workshop circle before curling into the fetal position and sobbing, past caring that twenty people were watching.

"This fear of abandonment is very strong, very powerful," Frances said to the group. "It is difficult to trust others, friends, lovers or partners. Our parents try hard but inevitably they fail. We must learn to parent ourselves."

That night when I flung myself onto my bed I landed on the teddy bear my FYP group had given me for my last birthday. At the time I'd been astonished at their choice. A forty-eight- year-old woman with a teddy bear?

"Everyone needs a teddy bear," they had said. I'd hidden it under a pillow in a corner of my bed.

Now I clutched it, weeping for the child I'd been. She'd had no security when she was honest, and not much more when she tried to be what other people wanted. Nothing had changed. I thought of Paul, whose love and acceptance had freed me to be myself. I had tried so hard to love him perfectly, and he had died anyway.

I sat at my window watching the stars, the bear damp under my chin.

CHAPTER 22
Homecare

It was a relief to creep back to Homecare on the Monday morning after Psychosynthesis Essentials. The Red-Suited Woman had still not returned, and I felt vulnerable and abandoned. Inhabited by that needy child, I suppose. I chose to clean bathrooms so I could be alone.

I put my blue basket of cleaning supplies on the edge of the bathtub, picked up the brush and the cleanser and began to scrub the toilet bowl. The wonderful part of Homecare, I'd discovered, was that I could work alone and think. The physical work of cleaning ran parallel to the mental process of scrubbing down the challenges of my life in the Foundation. Corinna, the blonde, German cellist who focalized the department, had been saying this all along, but it had taken me about three months to appreciate it. In fact, at the beginning I'd hated Homecare. Despite the angel of Purification, the same one as I'd had in Experience Week, I resented the invisibility of cleaning, felt humiliated by having to kneel to clean toilets, skirting boards, spots in the carpet. Eventually I got so frustrated that I burst into tears during a Wednesday afternoon attunement. I winced at the memory as I wiped the mirror clean.

"I don't love this work; I can't. I've barely made it to the end of the first month. I don't know how I can do it for a whole year," I'd said to them.

There was silence. I felt terrible. I liked Corinna, Mary and Jan so much and I was a failure. Corinna looked thoughtful.

"Is there one job you don't mind?"

I stopped crying and considered. Cleaning the sanctuary was okay. This was where we sang Taizé songs every morning, and I would sing while I worked there. It felt like a sacred space. I said this. Corinna nodded.

"Good. Then you will clean the sanctuary every week. It is a start."

It was a pity that the sanctuary was only cleaned once a week but then I realized that I enjoyed dusting and polishing the beautiful carved wood of the main and east staircases. The main stairs got a lot of use; they were cleaned three times a week, the other two staircases twice. I felt encouraged. Vacuuming, called hoovering here, was something I'd always disliked in Canada because of the noise. But here the sound effectively cloaked my voice so I could sing as I worked, without feeling self-conscious. Besides, the hoovers were Henrys, squat little machines, either red, blue, yellow or green, with a smiling face painted on the side. I liked them. Homecare had named each one separately. There was one Henry but there was a Henrietta, a Kermit, Grace, Patrick, Harald, the names went on and on. Each cleaning station had at least one hoover and Porter's Palace, the main station, had three. The day I accidentally knocked Henrietta down three stairs and apologized to her, I recognized that I was more connected to Homecare than I had thought.

So this morning, while I scrubbed the sink, I pondered the past year in the light of the revelations of the Psychosynthesis Essentials workshop.

The subpersonalities I'd experienced shouldn't really have been such a surprise. After all, hadn't I been aware of two sides of me ever since Paul's death? The vulnerable weeping woman and the tough, hard-working taskmaster? The workshop had just given me a sense of where they'd come from. With Paul there had been a third, the strong, loving woman, for whom life had been such a delight. The year before I'd left Toronto, Marilyn had shown me a fourth: a violent, raging neurotic. At least that subpersonality hadn't surfaced in the Psychosynthesis workshop.

I replaced the toilet rolls, emptied the garbage bin and began to wipe the edge of the bathtub. Whoever had used the tub last had cleaned it well.

Most of those subpersonalities had shown up in Homecare over the months. The Red-Suited Woman, naturally; she was the worker. The crying child subpersonality when I was still whimpering about the work. I straightened up from the tub, grabbed the hoover and sang "Dona Nobis Pacem" as I vacuumed the floor. We'd sung it in Taizé that morning. I wiped fingerprints off the door and ran water into the bucket to mop the floor.

At tea break (three bathrooms done, two to go), I put on a jacket and took my mug of English Breakfast tea and a slice of toast outside to a bench in the sunshine.

After a full year it seemed incredible to me that I had disliked Homecare for the first three months. I loved it now. I cherished the opportunities it gave me to think and understand what was going on in my life, "to purify on the inner as well as the outer" as Corinna said. Corinna modeled a combination of toughness and vulnerability that won my trust completely. She had been the one who persuaded me to share my difficulties openly with the other members of the department. Early on they had glimpsed the screaming subpersonality I associated with Marilyn. I closed my eyes in the sunshine and thought about Peter.

He'd been one of several long term members who took the trouble to welcome the new students into community life. I felt flattered when he singled me out at meal time. His enormous hands and bear-like body made me want to draw closer to him, for protection and warmth. Life in the Foundation had felt overwhelming at the start. I thought Peter might be an anchor that would keep me from losing myself.

But in the second week of the orientation month, Peter said casually at lunch time that a community woman he'd met on a weekend workshop was interested in him. I felt my heart sink. That very evening he'd invited me to go into town for a beer. I hesitated, but I agreed.

His blue eyes had glowed with warmth above the beer glass, blotting out the dingy pub.

"How did you come here to the Foundation?"

I told him about visiting Kate and Evan.

"So then you did Experience Week. Did you like it?"

"Not too much. I thought the place was weird."

"What brought you back?"

I told him how my family had lost its centre when my mother died, how my interest in life had disintegrated after Paul's death. I told him about everything except Marilyn. Whenever I stopped he asked more questions. It was curiously seductive, like someone undoing the buttons but waiting for me to take off the clothes myself. Eventually I had to duck my head to hide my tears from the other people in the pub. We left. He pulled me into an archway on High Street and held me. For once it felt safe to be so vulnerable.

Back at Cluny I blinked in the bright lights of the entrance hall. My eyes were sore, but I didn't want to say good night.

"Do you want to come up to my room for a tea and a cuddle?" he said.

I nodded. Smiled. I was still smiling when I left his room the next morning.

Two days later he told me he'd decided to make a commitment to the community woman.

"You fucking Judas," I had screamed at him in the middle of Cluny Woods. He listened, nodded, said we could still be friends. *Friends!* I was furious.

After she'd seen me in angry tears in the dining room, Corinna persuaded me to talk about Peter in the Homecare Department and exorcise my bitterness.

The department listened without judgment to my story.

"I thought it would be different here, in a spiritual community," I finished.

Corinna shook her head. "This place is a hothouse. Relationships spring up quickly, too quickly perhaps, and die almost as fast. I have seen this many times. I have lived it."

"It's the same here as everywhere," Mary added. "Women use sex to find love and men want to get laid."

I hung my head. Exactly what had happened.

"Ja. We *try* to be spiritual, but we are human," Corinna said. "We make mistakes. It is forgivable, I think."

I don't know what I would have done without Homecare. At my four month evaluation, I turned down an opportunity to move to another department because I'd learned to enjoy every aspect of the work. It felt like a miracle.

A cloud crossed the sun. Tea break was over. I took my mug and plate to the stillroom and returned to my bathrooms. "Dona Nobis Pacem" gave way to "Singt dem Herrn." My German accent was appalling, I'm sure, but I loved the rollicking rhythm and the way the melody soared and dipped. My voice ricocheted off the tiles as I bent to clean the next toilet.

CHAPTER 23
Taizé

Singing had been a wonderful surprise. There had not been any singing at Cluny when I was in LCG; it had begun while I'd been back in Toronto. Members and guests would gather for twenty minutes each morning to sing songs from the Taizé monastery in France, simple rounds and easy harmonies in a variety of languages. I loved to sing, but Kathleen had always rolled her eyes and asked me to stop at the chalet. So when I sidled into the sanctuary for Taizé singing the first time, I listened and hummed under my breath. Slowly I began to join in, singing softly so no one would hear. My resentment, anger, bitterness and grief dropped away for those twenty minutes, and I was swept up in the beauty of the harmonized voices. I stopped criticizing God, stopped feeling like a victim, stopped thinking and let the singing open my heart. Often I'd be in tears. This was joy, this was community, this was a spirituality I could feel and accept. Finally I'd found something I loved. I always went into breakfast in a good mood afterward, even when my own voice failed.

"Taizé singing is prayer twice over," one of the leaders said. "We can't go wrong."

I would sing the "Taizé Hallelujah" or "Jubilate Deo" when I rode the bus or hoovered the stairs, but only if no one could hear me. I treasured this amazing spiritual connection in Taizé singing; only my pitiful voice distressed me. Eventually I decided to take voice lessons with Belia from Holland, who worked in the Pottery. She had sung professionally in her pre-Foundation life. I thought three or four lessons would make a difference, help me to sing more easily.

The first lesson was in the music room in the Universal Hall in the Park. Belia walked around me looking me up and down. Then she made me walk around her.

"Posture is wrong. Bend the knees, drop the shoulders, open the chest, breathe. Breathe deep, from the diaphragm. No, belly, belly, you are breathing from the chest."

"Isn't that where my lungs are?"

"Your lungs are huge, they reach nearly to the pelvis. Breathe from down there."

My lungs felt nowhere near my pelvis, but I was breathing too hard to protest.

"Lie down on the floor." She pulled a huge rock out from a corner of the room and placed it on my abdomen. The tea and scone I'd eaten just before the lesson lurched in protest.

"Raise the stone with your breath. Up! Come on; it is not that hard."

By the time I staggered out, carrying the stone so I could practise breathing with it back at Cluny, I still hadn't sung a note. Not what I'd anticipated my first singing lesson would be. I signed up for more, hoping at some point my voice would come into it.

It was a slower process than I had expected. But I didn't eat before my next singing lesson, I learned to make the rock move on demand and I worked on my posture and breathing. Even though Belia still growled, I did start to sing. I couldn't hear much difference in my voice, but I enjoyed the lessons. Somehow I believed I would improve. Belia made me do bizarre exercises to "quiet" my body when I sang. One day Mary came into the laundry and found me standing among the sheets and towels, singing the "Taizé Alleluia" while rolling my shoulders and flapping my elbows. She burst into hoots of laughter.

"Are you trying to fly? You look like a drunken duck."

"Don't interfere with art."

The day Belia checked my range and pronounced me a mezzo soprano, I felt as if I were ready to join the opera.

The person I was when I sang Taizé was as close as I could

imagine coming to the subpersonality who had loved Paul so much. But most of the time I still felt like an uneasy jumble of parts, not an integrated whole.

CHAPTER 24
Authority Issues

For the first two months of my student year, Taizé singing had been my most positive connection to God in this spiritual community. Apparently it wasn't enough.

"This session is an opportunity to examine your relationship with God," the facilitator said to our FYP group at the start of an educational session in the third month, and I felt my heart sink. I could cope with God when I was singing. I could live with the constant reference to Him at the start of work shifts, just another aspect of the Foundation culture. But in all other situations He became an authority figure I didn't want to deal with.

Eight months later when I did the Psychosynthesis Essentials workshop, I would understand this reluctance much more clearly. God made me feel like a powerless child, and I didn't like it.

The facilitator said we'd use a "meditate and draw" approach as a way of sliding out of the conscious mind. I groaned inwardly. I felt inept when confronted with paper and pastels. No one ever expected artistic merit except me. But my lack of artistic ability was just an excuse, a distraction from the real issue. The truth was that I was always unnerved by any glimpse of what seemed to be hiding in my unconscious.

We meditated on our connection with God and then drew. My picture showed a towering thunderhead of cloud, bolts of lightning and a scowling, thin-lipped old God above the clouds, saying "NO." I was a little stick figure girl in the bottom corner. The child again. "God" looked like the angry Presbyterian minister from my childhood, even though my family had left that church when I was fifteen and we'd moved to Toronto. But here He was, resurrected from my unconscious. My FYP group stared in silence.

"How interesting that you've come here, to Presbyterian Scotland, to heal this view of God," said the facilitator.

I hardly heard her. No wonder I had trouble with spiritual authority, and forgiveness if I'd been carrying this view of God around all my life. Judgment and anger. I remembered the imposing church, with its dark carved wood and the blue panel with gold script high above the pulpit. "No Man Cometh Unto The Father But By Me." Beautiful but threatening.

I'd never felt good enough, always believed God would say no, whatever I asked. Well, He had, hadn't He? My mother and Paul were both dead, weren't they? I could feel my adult self vanish as tears surfaced. I clutched after a more mature response. God the Father meant patriarchy, male domination, women as second class citizens, as the cause of sexual sin. I'd hated the hypocrisy of "family values," the condemnation of other religions, even of other forms of Christianity. How could I heal?

"You could start by changing your language," said the facilitator. "Don't use 'God;' find an alternative that works for you."

I stared at her. I'd been an English teacher; I knew the importance of language. Why hadn't I seen this?

In the next meditation, I quietened my mind, until it was empty and waiting. Silently said "God." My muscles tightened automatically. I tried "Beloved." "Universe." "Mother." Nothing was quite right. It wasn't until I said "Spirit" into the silence that the tension eased. It seemed more neutral. I felt a trickle of gratitude in a sea of uncertainty.

CHAPTER 25
Allergies

Nothing changed quickly. When I paid attention, I used "Spirit." In my prayers, in my meditations, in the moments when I was trying to be a spiritual person. Whenever I focalized a Homecare shift I made sure I used "Spirit" in the attunement, and the shift felt much more grounded. When I was simply reacting, "God" leapt to my tongue, along with all the prejudices I had about religion, Christianity and authority in general. It was clear that the Red-Suited Woman part of me was a big reactor.

"Think of someone to whom you have a strong reaction, like an allergy," said Ben, as September rain streamed down the windows. My FYP group was having another education session, this time on conflict resolution. Ben was facilitating. I ran my mind over various people in the Foundation.

"Someone who makes you feel like breaking into an automatic rash as soon as they open their mouth or even walk into a room," he continued. "Someone to whom you have a violent response."

It was the word "violent." All the Foundation candidates fell away and I was back in Toronto with Marilyn. My stomach churned and the muscles tightened in my neck and jaw. I'd mentioned Marilyn once to my therapist, but otherwise I hadn't talked about her in the Foundation. I didn't want anyone here to know the person I became around Marilyn.

"Have you all found an example you can work with? Okay, ask yourself what rule that person breaks. What line does he or she cross that you believe shouldn't be crossed? What causes that automatic, allergic reaction in you?"

That was easy. Marilyn demanded my attention, insisted, pushed, pressured, beseeched, wouldn't hear no, wouldn't listen. *I'm suicidal; you're the only one who can help me; you made me love you.* She overwhelmed me with her neediness. Threatened to swallow me whole. I closed my eyes against the grey light, feeling a pulse throb in my temple.

"Where did that rule come from? Who taught it to you, either in words or by example?"

Taught me?

Ben's voice softened. "All our rules come from somewhere. Maybe they were never put into words; maybe we just absorbed them from the example of a parent, a teacher; maybe they were part of a family belief system."

Well, no one in my family was ever allowed to beg or beseech. Far from it. We were sent to our rooms when we had an emotion. I'd never been perfect; I still flushed with shame when I remembered the time I'd tried to toast my father's second marriage and burst into tears. But I couldn't think of many moments of failure. We coped; we endured; we were stoics. *We were fucking heroes.* I hadn't even begged Paul to live when he talked about dying. All right, I'd become ridiculously emotional since his death, but I never made the kind of demands on anyone that Marilyn had used to bludgeon me. Privacy and independence were cornerstones in my family culture.

"Picture what it would be like if you broke that rule."

If I became demanding, needy, clingy? People would hate me, as much as I hated her.

"If you broke it just a little," Ben added, reading my mind.

If I'd said to Paul - "Live. Please live. I need you"?

My throat ached at the thought. Grief surged through me. My eyes were still shut, but tears streamed down my face. I could not have put that pressure on him. If I'd said to my parents – but I could never have said what I felt to my parents. They made it so clear that they didn't want emotional scenes. Even when they put the family dog down, I wasn't told until afterwards and then by phone. I'd been in my twenties. A year and a half later I'd told God that I needed my mother to live. *God ignored me. I'm always ignored when I'm needy.* I was disintegrating. In a moment I'd be howling. I opened my eyes. There was a box of tissues nearby and I grabbed a handful. I wasn't the only one in tears. Ben waited until we were mopped up.

"We all carry a set of rules that we've internalized from childhood, and the stronger our obedience to a rule, the more we react when someone else breaks it." He paused to let that sink in. "When someone behaves in a way that we have never been permitted to behave, our reaction can look out of proportion to other people."

I stared down at my clenched hands, hearing Marilyn's social worker say, she's harmless, just pathetic; Jim say, be nice to her; my principal ask if I was overreacting.

I wasn't. She was completely out of control. Control matters. But then I remembered how I had wanted to mow her down with my car.

"When we have an allergic reaction to someone, it's worth checking to see why we're so upset. What rule of ours is that person breaking? Where does the rule come from? What would happen if we broke it? Lastly, is it still an important rule to follow? Maybe it doesn't have to carry so much emotional weight."

What would happen if I expressed my needs?

I can't. I can't do it. I'd be rejected. My needs were never met. Not by my parents, not by God. Only Paul met needs I didn't even know I had. And I met his because I loved him. But he died. He died. The one time I have my needs met he dies. I'm abandoned. That's what fucking well happens when I express my needs.

My chest felt tight with fear and rage. I was nearly back to the woman Marilyn had called into being in Toronto.

I left quickly at the end of the session.

The Red-Suited Woman was my armour. She could keep that angry, violent side in control and she could hide the needy child.

CHAPTER 26

Game Training

The Red-Suited Woman may not have made me feel very comfortable in community, but she shed a lot of light on the difficulties I'd had in my first year. I understood now why the Facilitation Training for the Game of Transformation had been so challenging.

It was Corinna who had persuaded me to sign up for the two week workshop eight months into my first student year, after I'd told her how much I'd learned from the Game of Transformation I'd done three years earlier.

"The facilitation training will deepen your connection to the Game and teach you how the Foundation works," she said. "It is the Mystery School in a box."

I couldn't resist.

I spent every free moment the week before the Game Training pouring over the manual. Between Homecare and study I was dead tired by the time the workshop began. The schedule for the two week Game training looked intense. Lectures in the morning, a Game every afternoon, and every other evening a discussion of different aspects of the Game.

"On the alternate nights you will have homework," said Angela, the Game Trainer. I wanted to go back to bed.

When we played Transformation Games in the afternoons, we took turns being player and facilitator. As players we were meant to be working with our own purposes, while supporting other players. As facilitators we kept track of the rules, which were many and complex, and kept tabs on the four players, their purposes, the patterns that surfaced in their games, their level of awareness, all of it. I needed a prodigious memory, a psychology degree and a doctorate in communication. I was supposed to be aware of my own emotions all the time too, although I had to stay detached from them when I was facilitating. But I couldn't be aware *and* detached; I didn't work like that. I needed to bury feelings. The more tired I was, the harder this became.

Now I know that as soon as I stepped into learning mode, the Red-Suited Woman moved front and centre, organized, task-oriented and focused. The problem was, the Game also demanded an emotional awareness, which wasn't part of her repertoire.

In my first attempt to facilitate four players in the Game, I felt as if I were holding too many strings at once. But Angela, the trainer, described my feedback to the players as laser-like, which sounded like a compliment, and she overlooked my mistakes. By the time I returned to my room that night, I was both elated and exhausted.

Two days later, I facilitated another game. Half way through it, one of the players drew a Setback card that read: "I just want to go back to the way things were." The player frowned as she tried to remember whether she had ever felt that way. Without warning Paul sprang to life in my heart; I wanted to fling myself across the Game board and howl for the past. I clenched every muscle in my body to stay upright and push away my grief and rage, but the laser-like qualities I'd demonstrated on Sunday vanished. So did Angela's compliments.

"You must not try to help players escape the pain. Pain is part of life and therefore part of the Game. Sometimes it is necessary for someone to experience their pain for several turns, even an entire game because they aren't ready to give it up, and that's what they have to understand. But it's their pain, not yours and it's their decision to let go, or not. Right?" She peered at my averted face. "What's the matter? Do you think pain is contagious?"

I didn't respond.

The next day, I was scheduled to play rather than facilitate. In an attempt to find a balance between thinking and feeling I made my Game Purpose an intention to be open to my feelings without judgment.

In the middle of the Game I got two Setbacks, which meant a Game Depression. "You are set back by your superiority" and "You are set back by your denial." Humiliating. I hated them both. The facilitator questioned me until I admitted that I felt superior about my facility with language and my ability to analyze situations.

"What I usually deny is my feelings of grief and sometimes anger. That might lead to migraine headaches. I get overloaded." Tears streaked my face.

"You are clear and quick at expressing yourself," said another player slowly. "But you're far more effective when you show your feelings. Then I can identify with you. When you just sit back and shoot words at me, I tend to shut down." The others nodded.

My strongest skill was not valued and my weakness was. I couldn't understand it.

Afterwards I got more feedback from Angela.

"I wonder if you are too focused on accreditation as a facilitator and not paying enough attention to your own personal process. You have personal issues coming up for you, like everyone else. You can't squash them down without repercussions. Those could come in the form of migraine headaches or in some other way that's more dangerous, an accident perhaps. You'll be a Game Facilitator, but you must take care of yourself."

I was too exhausted to take in what she said. Late that night, when I couldn't sleep and was writing in my journal, I thought back to the afternoon Game purpose, to be open to my feelings without judgment. I still hated being so emotional. Feelings got in the way of rational thought. Of articulation. Of ... of ... they just got in the way. Of course I denied them. They should know their place; instead they drove me mad, emerging like geysers at the most inappropriate moments.

During a lecture in the second week Angela talked about the Transformation Square.

"When a player lands on the Transformation Square, it means

that a major breakthrough connected with their purpose either has occurred or is ready to occur in their lives." She paused impressively. I shivered.

"Don't players – um - sometimes resist this?" I asked. "Leaving the old and familiar behind so suddenly feels – scary to me."

Angela merely gave me a blank stare and outlined the facilitator responses to the Transformation Square. Then she led a meditation in which she described transformation as a tunnel; behind was the familiar status quo, ahead was the new and we were to picture ourselves approaching the threshold of the new. I felt myself hesitating in that tunnel, reluctant to move forward yet knowing I had to. Angela's voice droned on, but I lost the thread. I had been in the transformation tunnel for eight years, ever since Paul's death, and I was reluctant, despite all the therapy and my months in the Foundation, to leave my old identity behind. It wasn't just Paul either. Teaching, family ... It was security, it was what I knew. I fought the urge to curl up in a ball. Eight years! How long was I going to hibernate? Tears seeped from under my closed eyelids.

I'd changed locations and jobs, but otherwise I was the same person I'd been in Toronto. I worked hard, denied my feelings, refused to take risks and clung to the rational, analytic, mind-based person I'd believed myself to be my whole life. I'd changed my environment but it wasn't enough. I – *I* - had to change. I opened my eyes. I had to quit teaching, resign, turn my back on Canada and commit to life in the Foundation. If the way back had closed, then I might change.

So here I was, a month into my second year, seeing the fragmentation of my personality much more clearly. I wasn't sure how I was going to integrate the bits and pieces, but it wasn't going to happen in Canada. It would have to be here, in the Findhorn Foundation.

CHAPTER 27

The Guest Department

Corinna lifted her wine glass in a toast to me, as I sank my knife into a rare steak. We were sitting by the fire in a Forres pub, which I visited whenever I couldn't cope with another healthy, vegetarian meal at Cluny.

"You should apply to focalize Homecare," she said. Corinna had left Homecare for another job ten months back but she continued to act as an informal mentor.

I frowned at her.

"Well if you won't, then you need to move on."

"I don't want to move. Jan can focalize. We work well together." I savoured the greasy onion rings.

"No. Homecare is an entry-level position unless you focalize. You have learned what you needed to learn there. This is how the Mystery School works; you stay in one job until you are so comfortable that you do not want to move, and then it is time to go."

"That's ridiculous." I jabbed impatiently at a mushroom, which skidded off my plate onto the floor. Corinna laughed.

"You know what happens if you ignore Spirit," she said. "You become unhappy where you are. For whatever reason the situation becomes intolerable. You need to move when you are called."

"But I'm not called anywhere."

"You will be."

I went up the bar and ordered a second glass of red wine.

Sure enough, Maureen from the Guest Department approached me a week later.

"We've got a vacancy coming up. Would you apply?"

"I don't think I'd be good enough, Maureen."

"You were good in the training in the spring," she said. "You'd be fine."

"I'll think about it."

"Go for it," Corinna urged. "You will learn a lot."

"What, exactly?"

"It is the next level. Holding guests in Homecare is easy. Holding guests in workshops will stretch you. Trust me. It is also rewarding."

I trusted her all right. I had a picture of myself struggling to learn a whole new set of skills, and learning suddenly felt overrated. But I didn't want to end up unhappy, leaving Homecare because it had become intolerable. Besides, I'd been a teacher for twenty-five years. I could handle groups. So I said yes.

Three months later I sat alone in the sanctuary, concentrating on my breathing. Once I'd breathed myself into calmness, I pictured a door in my heart, opening. I imagined allowing, holding, loving, praying. Without Paul it was hard work. I also reminded my Red-Suited Woman subpersonality to hibernate for the next seven days.

The learning curve in the Guest Department had been steep, just as Corinna had predicted. I knew now that before I met a group I had to make sure the teacher aspect of me had backed off far enough so that she didn't surface when I started to speak. I didn't want a repeat of my first week, when a guest had said acidly that I sounded as if I was talking to teenagers.

Fortunately new focalizers always worked with an experienced partner. Maureen, my co-focalizer that week, had said that I might want to tone down the "edge" in my voice that suggested I expected people to listen.

"It's a bit of a red flag to people with authority issues," she said. "We get the attitude anyway, but there's no point in inviting it."

I understood, and these were adults, not adolescents. But leading a group brought out the teacher in me. It was a Pavlovian response. I had assumed it would be my strength in Guest Department work, not a liability.

On my second day I'd just done a beautiful work attunement session, when Anthony, a middle-aged English businessman, stopped me on the way out of the sanctuary.

"I didn't come here to work. I'm on holiday. I'm sleeping in, not showing up in the kitchen every morning to cook," he growled.

"Didn't you realize you'd be working? It's in the brochure," I said.

"I guess I missed that. But-"

"This is a spiritual community, not a cruise ship. Working with members is the best way to see how we bring spirituality into everyday life."

"Don't expect me to pay, and work *and* be spiritual. It's not on," he said, and stalked off. I felt my blood pressure rising.

"It's fine, it's fine," Maureen said when I told her. "He's made a mistake, that's all. Come to the wrong place. The kitchen will survive if he doesn't show up. Don't pressure him, and he may change his mind."

He hadn't changed it Monday morning, when he wandered into the kitchen for the first time after mid-morning tea break. I fumed when I heard. Maureen grinned at me over her mug of tea in the Guest Department Office.

"Remind me what angel card you picked for this week," she said innocently.

"Love. My bloody angel is Love, as you know perfectly well. But that one – are you seriously telling me I should be loving that idiot?"

"'Should' is not a helpful word. But yes, we embody Foundation values, including love. The poor man probably works hard the rest of the year and really needs a holiday now, or sleep. He hasn't asked for his money back. He'll be getting something out of the week, whether he works or not. Anyway, look what he's teaching you."

"What? What is he teaching me?"

"He's showing you something about your own strong work ethic. How do you react when you can't measure up to your high expectations?"

I slumped in my chair. Thought about the times when migraines forced me to retire to my room and leave my work to others to complete. "Badly. I hate myself."

"Well, perhaps you can learn from Anthony. It's not about control, Experience Week. You tell people how it works here, and then you model it; you love them and pray for them."

"But if they were all like Anthony it wouldn't 'work' here at all."

"They aren't all like him. He is the only one in a group of twenty. *It's not about control.*"

I groaned. She laughed.

In fact, Anthony was intrigued by what others shared that night about their work experiences, and he did show up in the kitchen the next morning on time.

I felt as if I were being chipped away, like a block of stone. I was grateful for what I'd learned on the Psychosynthesis Essentials workshop. I could see the Red-Suited Woman had to go or at least be arm-wrestled into a back seat. There was no place for her in a group of adults in Experience Week. She was helpful with the organization beforehand, but she was a disaster with guests. Again and again I remembered the Multicultural Leadership Program, where I'd facilitated a group with Paul. Remembered how his sense of humour had buoyed us up all week, how easy-going, relaxed and accepting he'd been. How open.

Well, I didn't have him. I had my other co-focalizer and I had Spirit. I leaned heavily on both.

Maureen and other focalizers reminded me about mirroring. Every time I reacted to some guest or other I tried to remember to look at myself, see what part of me was like that guest. It was endless. Over the various guest weeks I faced every aspect of myself I'd ever disliked and quite a few I didn't recognize at all. Arrogant and judgmental people, overly emotional people, angry people, ultra-sensitive people, confrontational people, needy, attention-seeking people, dismissive people, people who dithered and couldn't commit, all of them trooped through my Experience Week groups, reminding me of me or shedding new light, to my disgust, on aspects of my character I hadn't seen before. A whole series of opportunities to grow.

I prayed daily, sometimes moment to moment. Asked for help, for a guest, for me, for my co-focalizer. Asked for the ability to love, to keep silent, to stay open. Often the energy of a situation changed in the few seconds it took me to center myself and ask for help. By the time I spoke, the situation had altered, or the person I was about to speak to had re-considered.

I prayed for patience the evening a young woman told me the reason she disliked me was that I reminded her of her step-father back in the States, and then sat there, apparently waiting for me to change. Another week, a guest spontaneously remembered early sexual abuse and cried for three days. I prayed for love, tried to picture it as an energy comforting and protecting her. It was hard work. Later my co-focalizer, Niels, suggested that she had felt safe enough in the group to let the memory of the past emerge.

"As you get better," he said, "the weeks often get more difficult, because of that increased safety factor."

"Harder than this?"

He laughed.

I learned not to take guests' attitudes personally. To maintain my sense of humour. One Wednesday morning on a group gardening project, a guest heard me cursing the couch grass I was weeding. Couch grass sends long roots in every direction and is almost impossible to eradicate.

"How can you be like that *here*?" she breathed, as if I had just trampled a religious icon in front of a believer. I shoved the trowel deep into the ground before answering. The Red-Suited Woman particularly disliked starry-eyed, New Age nitwits, and she was clamouring to give voice.

"Because 'here' is real, not some kind of spiritual fantasy land," I said finally, hurling a handful of couch grass into a container. "Sometimes I get fed up. If I don't express how I feel about the couch grass, I'll explode. I'm being authentic."

She looked as if she thought authenticity was overrated.

Over the months I watched guests come and go. Guests who came having lost a relationship, or a child, or a job; guests who had read about the Foundation but didn't know why they had come; guests whose faith and experience of Spirit made me feel like a beginner; guests like me, who knew their old lives weren't working and didn't know how to bring about a change or what change might look like. Guests who came in light-heartedly and discovered they were at risk of wanting serious change in their lives by the end of the week.

I witnessed the pain people felt when they tried to grapple with the principle of unconditional love and realized how little existed in their own lives. Some chose to focus on one particular person either in the group or in the Foundation instead of working with love as a general principle. Occasionally a guest developed a huge romantic attachment to my co-focalizer, which required very clear and gentle handling. I saw people fall genuinely in love and remembered loving Paul after three days of the Multicultural Leadership Program. I listened with anguish when a middle-aged, married church minister, who had come alone on the week, talked about his conflict after falling in love with a woman in the group.

"I have the angel of Integrity." He was close to tears. I never learned who the woman was but she had rejected him very gently, he said. In his completion he talked about his fear of returning home to what he now acknowledged was a loveless marriage.

My heart twisted inside me as I listened to him. I never saw him again, but I prayed for him.

I always had a week of preparation between guest weeks so burnout was held at bay. I learned that I could cope with almost anything for a week, but Friday nights after the celebration dinner I would take a long bath, then shut myself into my room alone to maintain balance. Because guest weeks could be a twenty-four-seven job, it was easy to feel separate from the community. Taizé helped. I sang every morning. I tried hard to reconnect on other levels every interim week. That was when I went to meetings, had tea or beer or a glass of wine with friends. I saw a lot of Stewart. He would always lend a sympathetic ear if I needed one.

So I wasn't very happy when a Japanese woman fell in love with him during her Experience Week. It wasn't one of my weeks. I only knew because she sat down at the lunch table with a group of us one day and encircled him with so much attention he couldn't interact with anyone else. A friend of mine who worked in the kitchen watched this and rolled her eyes. "She was like that the whole shift this morning. I didn't know whether to laugh or take a knife to her."

I wanted to hand her the knife.

One of my hardest weeks came just as war broke out in Yugoslavia. A Bosnian woman broke into tears as she introduced herself.

"I learn this morning there is fighting near my town," she said. "I am happy to be here, I have wanted this for years, but my husband and son – what is happening to them? If they are hurt or killed while I am safe here I cannot forgive myself. I am so afraid."

Hot tears welled up in my eyes. Glancing around the circle I saw that virtually everyone else was weeping or fighting tears, except for one woman in her forties who had pulled out a pen and notebook and begun to write. When the Bosnian woman finished, we called tea break. I pulled my Red-Suited Woman front and centre and intercepted the notetaker before she'd reached the door.

"Excuse me. An hour ago we all agreed to confidentiality. Why are you taking notes while someone is sharing?"

"I'm a writer. I take notes," she said, hostility in her eyes, her voice and the set of her shoulders.

"No. Not here. That is not how it is going to be. Either you put that notebook away and respect the agreement we've made, or you leave the workshop now. You will get your money back. Let me know at the end of tea break."

I used my iciest teacher glare and waited to hear that she was leaving but it didn't happen. I didn't see the notebook again, but she spent the week trying to needle everyone into confrontation and argument. My co-focaliser ignored her as did the other guests but I was in Red-Suited Woman mode all week long, afraid that the group would ignite World War Three. I didn't pray, didn't try to open my heart, didn't love. What did happen was that at the end, the group shed no tears, showed no particular closeness. They shared pleasant conversation and unemotional farewells.

That weekend I joined a workshop on Conflict Facilitation as a participant. The first session began with a quotation from Danaan Parry, the late author, conflict facilitator and environmentalist: "All conflict is a struggle toward intimacy."

"If you don't allow anger to surface," said Andrew, the facilitator, "no other genuine emotion will emerge either."

I was shaken. Once again I saw the impersonal ending of the Experience Week that had just finished. If I had stood back and allowed the conflict to come out, would the week have had more depth? Who had I really been trying to protect? I had a terrible feeling it had been me, not the guests at all.

I remembered Marilyn then, and my own out-of-control anger. Saw that my shield, the Red-Suited Woman subpersonality, was dedicated to control, to keeping everyone at arm's length. It wasn't necessarily a good thing.

My emerging spirituality got severely tested when Keiko, the Japanese guest who was infatuated with Stewart, returned to the Foundation for a three-week stay a few months after her Experience Week. I read her name on the guest list with dismay. I was picking up my dinner Friday night in the kitchen when she came flying in the back door, still wearing her coat, calling Stewart's name. He turned, serving spoon in hand, his chef's jacket streaked with gravy stains, just as she flung herself onto his chest and encircled him with a grip like an octopus. He staggered, laughed and hugged her. I turned my back on them and took my nut roast with mustard gravy into the dining room. It was one of my favourite meals, but that night I couldn't finish it.

When I learned that she planned to come back in another three months for LCG and the one-year student program, I ground my teeth. She had already shown she tolerated no outsiders, and

Stewart seemed okay with this. I was going to lose my best friend.

Fortunately there was still Taizé, which I was leading one day a week, since other people had moved on, and therapy, and the occasional Homecare shift.

I turned fifty that November. Apart from the decade change, I was struggling with an inflammation in the arch of my right foot. I couldn't stand without pain, and I felt more like eighty than fifty. One of my friends gave me a visit to a body therapist as a birthday gift so I made an appointment and talked about my foot.

"I feel trapped. My left foot has been arthritic for years, but I can cope with that. This is so much worse."

"Are you by any chance resisting moving forward in some way? Perhaps this is an energy for change of some kind that you are blocking?"

I hadn't even let myself consider that. I stared out the window.

"I'm a little tired of the Guest Department," I said at last. "It might be time to change jobs."

She nodded. "Stay open to possibility. It may be something even bigger. Meanwhile you might consider acupuncture for your foot."

I had two acupuncture treatments, and the foot problem cleared up completely.

Between Christmas and New Year, I had a dream.

I'm standing in an open space, looking at a log cabin. It's a sunny summer day, not too hot. The air is very clean. I'm in Canada. Behind the cabin is forest. Behind me is meadow, the green and gold grass rippling in the breeze. No one is around. There are no roads, no other buildings, no sign of other people. It's very peaceful.

I woke up. Knew. It was time to go back to Canada.

CHAPTER 28
To Go Or Not To Go

The more I thought about it, the more I was sure Spirit was wrong. This was no work department attunement issue. Canada was a place of grief and misery for me. Failure. Canada was the land of Marilyn and the Mr. Hyde side of me, the place where I couldn't meet the expectations of family and friends, where I'd been afraid I'd be unable to get out of bed because of the depth of my depression. Did Spirit really believe I could go there again, without a job or a home and be happy, be whole? In the Foundation, people were accepted, with their emotions, sub-personalities, doubts and ambivalences. I was a mess of bits and pieces, but I fit in here. Canada was like my family, who required a single entity with a happy face, a Red-Suited Woman.

I remembered the masks I'd drawn in the first week of my student program. The young face with the smiling mouth, worried forehead and frightened eyes; that was my Canada face. The second one, split in two, one side controlled, the other demented; that one had no place in Canada but she could exist here. I was nowhere near the third, the calm face lit by a rainbow. I wasn't ready for Canada.

But I could hear Corinna's voice in my mind. "You know how the Mystery School works. You stay in one place until you have learned what you needed to learn and you are comfortable. Then it's time to move. If you don't, it will become intolerable."

I wasn't ready. But that didn't mean it wasn't time.

"All right, I'll go," I said aloud to Spirit. "But in June. Six months. The day after the Solstice."

There were no more dreams.

I told Jan and Stewart, and then the people in the Guest Department. They looked dismayed but didn't say much. It's hard to argue with someone's guidance. Meanwhile I signed up for The Mastery, a weekend workshop I'd wanted to take ever since arriving in the Foundation.

The workshop required a three minute performance piece. I was going to sing. I'd been taking singing lessons for three years and leading Taizé for almost two. I could do this. I chose "I Dreamed A Dream" from *Les Mis*. It was well within my range and I liked the song. I'd felt lots of sympathy for Fontine, the character pregnant and abandoned by her lover, who becomes a prostitute to support herself and her child and dies early in the production. I took it into a singing lesson to get some coaching and later I practised in the ballroom with my friend Wendy, who had also signed up for The Mastery. She was singing "Cry Me A River."

"I love this song," she said during a break one practice. "I'd like to remind everyone of Billy Holiday, you know, smoky and sexy."

I smiled. Wendy had a voice as high and pure as a choir boy.

"I'd like to make everyone cry," I said, remembering how often singing had moved me to tears. "Sing it that perfectly."

"We'd better practise more."

The workshop began on Friday night. By performance time Saturday afternoon, I was tired and cranky from a late night and the stress of the morning. I wanted nothing more than a cup of tea and a piece of cake, by myself, in a cafe overlooking the sea. Instead I was locked up in a windowless room in the Universal Hall with twenty other performers and a crowd of assistants to the workshop facilitators. My name was called third.

"What do you want us to get from your performance?" asked the facilitator. I cleared my throat.

"Well, I – I hope you'll feel the pain of the loss, you know, of a dream." I found my note and began. It seemed so high that I stopped, checked and began again.

I'd never sung solo outside of the shower and music lessons. I could hear my voice rasping, thinning, clawing at the notes like a mouse in a trap. Breath vanished; every word hurt; the song was interminable. When my voice actually cracked on a high note I wanted to disappear. At the end, I sat in silence.

"How did that feel?" asked the facilitator.

"Awful. It was my worst nightmare," I said, tears spilling inexorably down my face. "And this song is so sad." I'd been practising for a month, and this was the first time I'd really heard how painful it was.

"Say the words aloud this time, don't sing."

Don't sing? Humiliated, I took a deep breath and began to speak. I'd never said the words aloud before. Without the notes, they didn't come easily. I had to search my mind to retrieve them. The result was I really heard them for the first time. By the time I'd reached the third line – "I dreamed that love would never die" - I recognized for the first time that I was singing my own story.

I got the words out, slowly, in the right order, with long pauses as grief and memory overwhelmed me. Tears dripped from my chin and jaw into the neck of my sweater. When I finished at last, I sat, staring down at my hands, stunned by my blindness. My story set to music, and all I'd been aware of were the notes.

"Look around you," said the facilitator. "Make eye contact with everyone."

I raised my head. I could barely see them in the shadows but their faces gleamed silvery, wet. I saw tissues. Everyone was crying. Every person was in tears. Just what I'd said I wanted. I stumbled back to my chair, desolate amid the applause.

The following Saturday I took Belia out to tea to drown the taste of failure. I ordered a shortbread, Belia had a scone. I could see the question in her eyes as she wrapped her hands around her cup.

"The part of me that sings-" I fought to keep my voice steady, "never heard how sad that song was until then. I was awful. They didn't applaud me because I sang well; they felt sorry for me when I cried."

Belia frowned. "No, no, I do not believe it was like that. You have not performed a solo in public before. Performance anxiety tightens up the whole system. And the sadness, well, I wonder if you are so focused on perfection and performance that you automatically push away the emotions."

I was already so upset that it took very little to bring tears. I swallowed half a cup of scalding Earl Grey tea, and stared at the tabletop.

"When I was performing regularly," Belia went on, "I used to find that I had to rehearse a new song for about three months before I sang it in public, in order for me to experience whatever feelings the song brought up. Experience them and then sing them with the notes. Perfection is a cold thing; it does not move an audience. I have said this to you before. Emotion does." She spread strawberry jam on her scone.

"Yes, but when I feel a lot I can't sing at all. I can barely speak."

"Indeed. But you do not overcome that by stopping the breath, which is your usual response."

"Not the breath lecture, Belia, please. I can't cope."

"Ideally you need to be able to feel it all and convey the feeling as you sing the notes. Feel it, not shut it down. That takes time. Then, with the breath flowing properly, you will feel *and* sing at the same time."

"But ..."

"Singing *is* feeling. In the Mastery you may not have been able to sing well, but the people were moved by your feelings, your grief. By your sense of loss, which you conveyed very powerfully and courageously. They did not applaud out of pity."

It couldn't be that simple. I went up to the counter, got more napkins, ordered a second pot of tea and another shortbread. If I couldn't get through speaking the words of a song, how was I going to leave the Foundation? I wondered if I could decamp in the middle of the night.

Stewart had said little about my plans, but one day, after I'd asked him to drive the bus for my Experience Week group, he stood up and put his arms around me.

"Don't go back to Canada. You're my best friend; I love you. Stay." He held me so tightly I couldn't see his face. I hugged him back. For a moment I wanted to forget everything I knew and melt. Then sanity reasserted itself. His wife still expected him in Glasgow every seven or eight weeks. His Japanese girlfriend would be resurfacing soon. Nothing had changed, even if his words made my heart sing.

"I can't. I don't know why, but I have to go."

His arms dropped and he turned away.

Sure enough, Keiko arrived on schedule on April 1. As soon as she landed, she latched onto Stewart like a wet T-shirt and scowled every time she saw me. At first I tried not to let her make a difference. One night in mid-April, I joined him for a late night cup of tea in his room. He was sitting up in bed reading through a play he'd written years ago. I lay down next to him and balanced the mug of tea on my stomach. The script was hilarious; he read all the characters in different voices and I laughed so hard the tea slopped onto my shirt. I suppose we were making a lot of noise. Without warning, the bedroom door crashed open. Keiko stood on the threshold, her dark eyes tragic and accusing. We stared back, without moving, a frozen moment in a French farce. No one spoke. Then she said to him: "I need change for a phone call."

He scooped a handful of change out of a drawer in his bedside table. She took it and walked away, slamming the door behind her.

I sat up. "Stewart, what's going on? Am I suddenly not supposed to be here?"

"Ach, no. It's fine. I told her I didn't want to see her tonight. Don't worry. I'll talk to her."

"*Talk to her*," I echoed in disbelief. "But … she's mad. Obsessed. She's not here for spiritual reasons. She's only here for you. How are you going to change that by talking to her?"

"She's just a friend." He picked up the play again and began to look for where he'd left off, clearly not about to discuss it.

I left a few minutes later. Outside in the corridor I hesitated, feeling the hairs on my neck lift as if I were being watched. But I'd closed his door; it would be ridiculous to go back now. I glanced around the empty hallway and open staircase up to the floor above. No one. I headed toward my own room, without looking up to the second floor corridor. Maybe she was up there, waiting to see me leave, before returning to confront him. Even so, I couldn't fight on that level, like two dogs snarling over a piece of meat.

Within days my relationship with Stewart turned wooden and lifeless. Without the laughter and friendship we'd shared for three years, I was desolate. I remembered Corinna's words again. "It's time to move. If you don't, life will become intolerable."

I had agreed to move, but on my schedule, not Spirit's and it was too late to change now. I'd booked a flight for June, and my work schedule was full. I struggled on.

In the end I decided to trust the process. Completion was an important part of life in the Foundation. I would do this right. I asked Jan to hold my leaving meditation. We were having tea in Forres. She put her cup down and looked at me.

"How are you doing this? You seem so calm and it's such a big step."

"I don't believe it's happening," I said. "I just don't believe it's all coming to an end. But when I let myself dream into it a bit, I wonder what Spirit has in mind."

"Do you have any plans?"

"I'm not staying in Toronto. I've decided to head out into the wilderness, like my dream. I'm going to buy a secondhand camper van and drive west. Rediscover my own country. There's no point in trying to fit back into a life that's disappeared. I'm going on."

Her eyes were huge but she didn't speak for several minutes. "I keep thinking I'll get used to saying goodbye to people, but I never do."

I gulped down my Earl Grey tea, trying to swallow my sadness.

I set up a series of formal goodbyes.

"I'm frightened," I said in my last therapy appointment with

Elke. "I'm following the guidance I got in that dream, but I have the terrible fear that God's going to ask the impossible of me when I'm in Canada."

"Follow your guidance but set some boundaries. Why not warn God you'll go but you'll allow one year or six months or whatever to get clear what the point is? If at the end of that time, you can't see any valid reason to be in Canada, tell God you're coming back."

I gazed at her in admiration and felt almost cheerful.

I was "tuned out" of the Guest Department.

I asked for a leaving table and booked the sanctuary for a Taizé evening. I was enormously grateful to see how many people came from the Park. The kitchen and dining room people made spaghetti with tomato sauce, garlic bread and salad, and decorated the massive T-shaped table they had set for me. I'd bought three bottles of wine and three bottles of non-alcoholic drink, and more bottles appeared like the miracle of the loaves and fishes.

At the end of the meal four Taizé singers came up to me. The dining room fell silent. Carin spoke. She was Australian, freckled and sang Alto.

"When you were away on holiday in April, the Taizé singers got together and made a tape, with the four parts of all your favourite songs, coming in one at a time just the way we do it in the sanctuary. You'll still be able to sing in harmony with us when you're in Canada."

The dining room broke out into cheers and applause. I took the tape in trembling fingers. There was a black and white photo of Cluny on the front, the list of songs on the back and inside, the names of all the singers in the various sections, from bass to counter-tenor. I could hardly take in what I was seeing. Carin shushed everyone and the four of them sang "Surrexit Christus," my favourite Taizé song, in four parts. As they began it for the second time, people stood and sang with them. I managed to whisper thank you, hug the four singers and wave.

On my last night Jan led the leaving meditation for me in the sanctuary with about thirty people. Corinna brought her cello and played Bach. I could feel the deep resonant notes of the cello reverberate in my heart. The music led into the meditation. After twenty minutes, Jan opened the space for people to speak. Stewart leaned forward, fixed his brown eyes on me and cleared his throat.

"I look at you and remember three years of friendship, support and love. And the special moments too. The cups of tea and pints of beer. All the laughter. Those bouquets of flowers we made up when you decided you wanted to practise flower arranging. We left bouquets of flowers all around Cluny. It was sunny that afternoon. I'll think of sunshine and flowers and laughter when I remember you."

Corinna's face was calm but her eyes glimmered.

"All the problems you had in the beginning in Homecare – they made me a better focalizer. I really felt like a success when you decided to stay."

Others chimed in.

"You've shattered two sacred cows for me. You've shown me how much fun there can be in being judgmental, and you make me wonder why you or anyone would listen to Guidance that's so obviously counter-productive. For you and for us."

People laughed out loud at the word 'judgmental.' I winced. Not enlightened after all this time. I was going to have to release that ambition.

"I am always surprised how you manage to be so direct about what you do not like without hurting people. I wish you could stay long enough for me to learn this from you."

"I am so proud that you have graduated from barely making a sound when you started to sing to leading Taizé here at Cluny. A lot of emotions come up for people when they do the breath work and sing, and you never let any of it stop you. I bless you with music in Canada. Find a group to sing with; tell them you are a soprano; do not give up."

"I've loved your humour. And your commitment in the Guest Department. I admired the way you struggled to be the best you could be every single week you focalized, no matter what you encountered."

At last I looked around the sanctuary.

"When I came here as an LCG in 1996, someone told me that I'd need to stay a very long time to fix all my problems. I was angry at the time, but she had a point. It's been more than three years, and enlightenment is obviously still a long way off. I'm both quite changed and not changed at all. Living here has been like being a rock on the beach, constantly pummelled by the tides and the wind and the other stones. I feel ground down, closer to my essence." To my surprise my voice was steady.

"You've all been part of the pummelling process, you and the work departments, the workshops and the guests. The day-to-day living in community with all the awareness that we can't avoid, even when we want to. I feel scrubbed and purified and reduced. Less baggage, I hope. I'm grateful, for the laughter, the tears, the friction and the grace. Most of all for the love." My face was wet with tears but I spoke clearly. "I guess the changes will continue in Canada. But it won't be the same without you."

I left just after lunch the next day, June 22. Four friends had offered to drive me to the train station. Almost everyone in the Cluny family lined up outside the house in a semicircle to hug me goodbye. The Homecare Department stood on the dining room roof and waved towels.

At the station the four of them heaved my huge suitcase onto the train and sang "Confitemini Domino" – Give thanks to the Lord – from the platform, belting out the delicate harmony, as the train began to move. People in the seats near me stared and then looked away when I caught their eyes.

I turned to the window, very nearly put my nose against it, watching the landscape flow smoothly past me on the way to Glasgow. I didn't even cry, determined not to miss a second in case I never saw Scotland again.

CHAPTER 29

Oh, Canada

It took me a month to pack Sam, my secondhand camper van, and find the courage to leave Toronto. In the third week of July I finally drove north. Late in the afternoon I pulled into a campsite in Kildare Provincial Park on Georgian Bay. I washed away the grime and sweat in the cold clear water, hung my bathing suit and towel on the clothesline I put up and made tuna salad for dinner. The sky was gold and peach. Pine trees surrounded the campsite. I heard families nearby, kids chattering with parents, squabbling with each other. The birds that had been chirping and rustling in the trees grew still. As I finished my tea, the whine of mosquitoes drove me into the van.

I enjoyed the solitude after living in community, but I could feel loneliness like a chill just under the surface. I meditated, asked for a blessing on my journey, and lay awake for a long time.

The days fell into a pattern. I drove north and west, watching for wildlife, checking into provincial parks at night, swimming at least once a day. I bought wild blueberries from roadside stands and ate them at every meal. The scenery was familiar from camping and boating with my parents and later with Paul: rock and pine trees, water, blue skies, sunsets. This was my attempt to trust Spirit enough to follow its guidance. Did I have the faith, the courage to stand alone, maintain my connection with Spirit, love myself enough to embrace a new life? I felt frightened but resolute.

I meditated in the mornings, sensed the familiar drop into a deeper, silent space, the connection with the part of me that is timeless. I sang with the Taizé tape whenever I couldn't get a radio station. It was fine during the day, lonely at night. I wrote, letters on my laptop and reflections in my journal.

Guidance. I'm driving across Canada alone because I had a dream of wilderness and thought Spirit was telling me to go back. Whatever happened to that logical, practical, analytic woman I used to be? The teacher, the daughter, the wife. Dad doesn't recognize me. Paul probably wouldn't either. Even I don't.

The migraines, the bone disease, the arthritis. Were they guidance? I didn't see that then. I saw them as warnings. I'd have developed something worse, cancer maybe, if I hadn't made real change. Like Mum, dead at 52.

Of course, I'm not 52 yet; I may die on this bloody trip. I still have migraines and arthritis.

One step forward, two back. In Winnipeg I stopped for a week and visited Paul's sister Mary. Paul and I in our wedding finery gazed down from pictures on Mary's walls, as if we had a lifetime to be together. I looked at the pictures and grieved him all over again, tears splashing down through my fingers onto my journal, into my pillow. Eleven years since he'd died. The unfairness of it still stung.

In desperation, I found an Internet cafe and wrote endless e-mails to Foundation friends. Perhaps by the time I'd reached the next city they would have responded.

When I set off from Winnipeg, I tried to embrace adventure and a new start again. I visited Neepawa, the childhood home of Margaret Laurence, one of my favourite Canadian writers. That night, in Riding Mountain National Park, I opened my laptop and stared at the screen. I'd read and reread the small collection of books I'd brought with me. *Bird in the House*, a book of Laurence's short stories, was one of my favourites. Could I write a short story? It was a good time to try. Slowly I began to tap the keys, seeing a ten-year-old girl whose family didn't understand her. Ellie, auburn hair and freckles. I wrote for two hours that night and was still thinking of Ellie in the morning.

As I headed west Manitoba grew flatter, the trees thinned, and I was on the prairie. The land was richly coloured and textured with a huge expanse of sky. I saw hawks everywhere and grain fields golden with sun. In Saskatoon I looked anxiously for e-mails from Foundation people. There were never enough and nothing from Stewart. My attempts to meditate often ended in tears of self-pity.

As light faded in the evenings, I finished reading my ten books for the second time and struggled with writing the story. I didn't have the discipline to write short stories, but Ellie felt very real to me. What I'd written was more like the beginning of a novel. The whole idea of writing a novel was preposterous, but I felt restless every evening until I slipped into my make-believe world. Ellie became seventeen, in her last year of high school. She wanted to leave her small, Northern Ontario town and study to be a vet at university. Her parents hoped she would settle for a nursing program in a local community college as her mother had done.

It never occurred to me that my new world was an internal one, opening through writing.

August was ending when I reached the mountains. One morning there was an icy skin on the surface of the water bucket.

Okay, I've followed my guidance this far. It's time for You to kick in. Where am I supposed to winter? Help me!

At the end of September I looked around my log cabin, high on a ridge a mile south of Quesnel in the interior of British Columbia. My furniture filled the living room, bedroom and kitchen. There was forest behind and open space with tall grass in front. Neither the road down below the ridge or my only neighbour to the east was visible. I'd seen bear scat behind the cabin and eagles overhead. It was just like the cabin in my dream nine months ago.

I remember that year in visual pictures of surpassing beauty, underscored by loneliness. I'd missed wilderness in Scotland and found it full strength back in Canada, in my drive west from Toronto and all around the log cabin outside of Quesnel.

But I was also looking for people, for community, for something to match the Findhorn Foundation. Because I was missing it so much, I signed up for a three week return visit in a year's time, which helped. I'd go back for the Sex and Spirit Conference, which had intrigued me when I'd heard about it in the early planning stages.

I didn't make friends in Quesnel. None of the kind strangers with their small-town conservative attitudes could warm me. I tried my best not to judge them while maintaining my own integrity, refused to join them in condemning pregnant teenagers, minority groups or people on welfare. They weren't upset.

"You're from Toronto," they said. "You could not be expected to understand that it's different here."

I tried, they tried, but I was too foreign.

I didn't think about leaving, not yet. I'd been sent here, or so I believed. There must be a reason. I decided to do volunteer work and chose the SPCA, thinking I might do better with animals than people.

The shelter, a small building set in a field surrounded by chain link fence, was just down the road from the town dump. I walked in the front door. A cat in a travelling case stared at me from the counter. The woman behind it faced her computer. Her name tag read Joanne. She didn't look up for several minutes. Eventually I cleared my throat and said I was interested in being a volunteer.

"All volunteers start at 8:30. The work is done by now."

I glanced at my watch. 10:30. "Could I come tomorrow, then?"

"All right. Fill in this form."

"Can I look around?"

"If you want. Don't touch any of the animals without washing your hands before and immediately afterwards."

I couldn't see any place to wash my hands.

Directly across from the counter a small room was alive with cats. Each cage had a typed label stating the cat's age, sex, and date of admittance. Green, yellow, blue and amber eyes gazed at me. The temptation to touch them was overwhelming. I backed out.

When I went down the hall into the dog area, every dog ran to the front of its enclosure and flung itself against the wire, barking frantically. The din was appalling. I forced myself to walk along the hall and look into each run. Lab crosses, Dobermans,

Rottweilers, one pit bull and a couple of Border collie crosses. I walked back, slowly, so the dogs wouldn't think they had chased me out.

"I'll be here tomorrow morning."

Joanne nodded. I pointed to the cat in the travelling case. "Is it being adopted?"

"No. Her time's up. She's being put down. We need the room."

Shocked, I looked into the case. The cat was a shorthaired tabby, immobile, except for her eyes.

"How old?"

"Two. Female, not spayed but she's had her shots. Would you like to see her?" Joanne's voice had turned pleasant at last. I nodded. She opened the door and scooped out the cat. I extended my finger for the cat to sniff, then rubbed her under her muzzle.

An hour later, I'd spent a small fortune and I was at home with Anna the tabby. She spent her first afternoon hidden underneath a bookcase in the unfinished basement.

I volunteered at the SPCA three mornings a week and felt my heart expand when I worked with animals. But they also underlined my isolation. At Christmas I hired a teenager to look after Anna and flew to Vancouver to spend two weeks with my aunt, with Kate and Evan and their daughter, Emma. They had all spent time in the Foundation and understood what I was missing.

My New Year's resolution was to continue the novel I'd begun in the summer. Time to resurrect Ellie and her family.

When I returned to Quesnel there was snow on the ground. Anna twined around my legs, purring.

I stopped worrying about loneliness. When I wasn't working at the SPCA, I wrote. I created a second major character, Rosemary, a forty-year-old widow.

The working title of my novel was *No Safe Place*, and the theme was the need to live fully, rather than hide and avoid life. Rosemary was Ellie's neighbour, an ex-teacher, who had left Toronto and moved to this small town to "recover" from her husband's death. Actually Rosemary was running away. She drank too much and had sex with a variety of unsuitable men. Rosemary tutored Ellie in English and they slowly formed a friendship that was threatened by their mutual interest in Kevin Wainwright, Ellie's sexy English teacher. As Ellie and Rosemary faced one crisis after another, life began to look up for me.

I dreamed about plot development at night, wrote daily for three or four hours without noticing the time pass and felt happy. Eventually I created Matt, a boyfriend for Ellie. He had Paul's patience and sense of humour and Stewart's husky build.

In March the SPCA hired me as a part-time kennel worker, to feed the animals and clean the cages. The money would pay for my trip to the Foundation's fall conference. I rescued a second cat from execution. Max was white, male and long-haired, everything I normally tried to avoid in cats. But he charmed me. While he and Anna spat at each other, the English teacher in *No Safe Place* lashed out at Rosemary because of her drinking. Ellie's father disapproved of her relationship with Matt, and after a huge blow-up, Ellie decided to leave home for good.

By the time I had completed the first draft of the novel it was late summer. Standing on the concrete floors at the SPCA had inflamed the arthritis in my feet until I could barely walk at the end of a workday. The animals were still heartbreaking, and I still had no friends. I worked my last shift in early September.

The day I left there was no card, no recognition of my months of volunteering, the cats I had paid to have neutered, or my willingness to fill in whenever needed. The shelter staff barely looked up when I turned in my keys. I went home in tears.

I was fighting a cold and revising another section of *No Safe Place* two mornings later, my nose red and swollen, when the phone rang. My Aunt Jane sounded anxious and far away.

"I wondered how you were doing with this nightmare. I just wanted to hear your voice."

"What nightmare?" I was preoccupied with Ellie's break up with Matt. My heart was aching for them.

"You haven't …? Turn on the television. The world as we know it is ending."

It was September 11, 2001.

For three days I watched the Twin Towers collapse over and over again, my eyes as red as my nose. The presence of Spirit didn't penetrate my desolation. Then CBC interviewed Americans trapped at airports in Goose Bay, Newfoundland and Vancouver, B.C. All of them said the same thing.

"Everyone has been wonderful, I'm so grateful, but I just want to go home. I need to go home."

That's what I want. I don't want to stay here in an alien place. Where is home for me? As soon as I asked, I knew. The Findhorn Foundation. They would be meditating and praying together, seeking Spirit in themselves, in desperate survivors, angry terrorists and frightened politicians. They would be talking about their feelings and listening to each other.

Yearning for the Foundation overwhelmed me.

Had I failed in my attempt to follow guidance? I pushed the thought away. Time enough to consider that question later. I began to pack.

Two weeks later I headed to Scotland to see whether I could go home to stay.

CHAPTER 30
Return

As I boarded the plane from Vancouver to London, bubbles of excitement like champagne rose from my belly. I tried to push them down. To hope so much was frightening. I had been guided to leave the Foundation, after all. What if Spirit refused to let me return?

"You look happy," said the ticket agent sourly in the London train station.

"Oh well," I grinned but tried to keep my voice casual. "I'm on a three week holiday."

"You know it's raining?"

"Not where I'm going."

He looked suspicious. In fact I had no idea what the weather in Scotland would be. But I felt as if it couldn't rain.

I took the bus from Inverness to Forres, twining my fingers together in an effort to still my excitement and drinking in the familiar landscape, the blue gray waters of the Moray Firth. Sue, who had once facilitated my Life Purpose workshop, met me at the bus stop. She held out her arms. I dropped my suitcase and hugged her.

"How was your trip?"

"Tell me the news," I said, at exactly the same moment.

One coffee later I knew who had left, what the current conflicts were and how the Sex and Spirit conference, which I'd signed up for, was shaping up in the aftermath of 9/11.

"Chaotic. So many American cancellations. I think they're afraid to fly."

"How's Stewart?"

"Getting a divorce at last. And he's in Barbados. His brother-in-law was in a car accident, and his sister asked him to come over and help her. Keiko went with him. They'll be back soon."

The dregs of my coffee went down the wrong way. I had to drink a glass of water to recover.

"Do you know why Spirit sent you back to Canada?" Sue asked.

"No. I did write a novel, but I don't imagine I had to go back for my own deathless prose." I paused, hearing myself. I was no Shakespeare, but I was happy writing. "I appreciated the peace and quiet for a while, but it was lonely. I was so different from the people around me. But I survived. I kept my connection to Spirit and didn't – well, twist myself out of shape, just to fit in. I must be stronger than I thought. Maybe that was the point. But it was a trial. I'd like to come back here to stay ... if ..."

She squeezed my hand.

There was a vase of sweet peas on the dresser in my room. I was home.

On Monday I was asked to work in the dining room for the week. I had just agreed when I heard my name. Stewart stood in the doorway of the dining room, his face split by a delighted smile, his arms wide. I flung myself into his embrace.

"Come and have a cup of tea. It's great to see you."

In the fifteen minutes that followed he didn't mention Keiko once. Finally I did.

"Oh aye, she's fine. She'll be here for dinner."

"Ah."

Later I sat in the shadowy sanctuary with its flickering candle and tall plants greening the bay window. I felt horribly vulnerable. *Can I come back? Give me a sign while I'm here, please.*

During the days that followed I went to Taizé singing, worked shifts in the dining room and meditated. To cover all bases I requested an interview with Karin from S&PD, the personnel department in the Foundation, and asked if there was space for me.

"You can certainly come back as an ex-member for three months. If a staff position opens up you can stay longer." She looked at me. "Why are you hesitating?"

"Spirit. I had guidance to leave in 2000. I want guidance to return."

I had still not received an answer by the time the one-week Sex and Spirit Conference began on Saturday. I'd been celibate for ages. I wasn't going to fit into the conference at all. But I'd made my reservation over a year ago, knowing that the energy of every conference impacted the Foundation and curious to see what would happen.

Conference presenters offered sessions on Tantric sex, healing and deepening long-term relationships, spirituality and sexual experience, spirituality and celibacy. Cluny was alive with sexual energy. When I went to bed Saturday night I heard moans, laughter and suggestive murmurs through the thin walls. I lay in bed listening, grimly at first, and then I began to smile. The first night of the Sex and Spirit Conference sounded like a success. Good for them. No doubt they've all prayed first, I thought as I punched my pillow into a comfortable shape and drifted off to sleep.

The program two nights later in the Universal Hall featured an ex-priest named Michael Kelly. He sat on stage with a small table beside him, on which a candle burned. A single light focused on him while the audience sat in shadow, and the effect was one of intimacy. I could hear the soft Irish blur in his voice when he spoke, as simply and directly as if he were talking to an Experience Week group of twenty instead of three hundred people in the Universal Hall.

"I knew from a very young age that I had a strong call to God. In Ireland, if you're a man born Catholic, that means entering the priesthood. I never had any doubt that I was meant to be a priest. My parents were delighted; I was the son for the Church. But when I reached thirteen or fourteen, puberty, I became aware of my sexuality, my interest in other boys. Of course it ran completely counter to the teachings of the Church as well as to my culture.

So I worked to deny it, to be celibate in heart and mind as well as body. I prayed and meditated and took cold showers and exercised. I did everything I could to repress it. I asked for help, but the Holy Fathers had nothing to offer beyond more of what I was already doing. I became a priest in those years, still fighting to repress my sexuality. And failing. Always failing. At last in my mid-twenties, I asked myself why God had chosen to call me to Him having given me such a strong sexual urge. The two weren't compatible, and I was unable to deny either one of them. I was a battleground. Eventually I began to wonder whether I needed to explore my sexuality since I couldn't shut it down. Trying to repress it had accomplished nothing. Perhaps I needed to take the opposite approach."

There was a long silence. Shadows flickered across Michael Kelly's face. The audience was still.

"I left the priesthood and I left Ireland." His voice held neither defensiveness nor bravado. "For the next years I travelled and then settled in Australia. I explored every aspect of my sexuality that occurred to me. I spent time in bathhouses, in bars, on city streets. I had one-night stands, multiple partners, anonymous sex and group sex. Everything I thought of, I tried."

He paused again. The darkened hall was soundless, as if everyone had stopped breathing.

"And in every place, no matter how dark, I found grace. God was always there, everywhere I went, whatever I found. There was God. Eventually I came to believe that it is better to be whole than to be good." He looked around the hall and then lowered his head.

A gay friend turned his head to speak to me and saw my clenched hand pressed to my mouth, my shaking shoulders, my face streaming tears. He held my free hand for a few minutes, then passed me a tissue. I couldn't speak. When the lights came on I stumbled out of the hall and onto the bus to Cluny, still hearing: "In every place, no matter how dark, I found grace. I found God."

I don't remember praying that evening when I went to bed, or dreaming of transformation of any kind, but when I woke up in the morning I had changed. I had accepted the Foundation men that I'd previously criticized for their use of women and their apparently casual sexual encounters. For once that morning I had no judgment. Somehow during the night, I had let go of the expectation that everyone needed to believe and behave as I did.

I'd struggled my whole life to be perfect, in my family, in my job, here in the Foundation, and I'd never achieved either perfection or peace, except for the short time with Paul.

Could it possibly be enough to be whole? Was this the guidance I'd been waiting for?

CHAPTER 31

The Mystery School Revisited

I did it. I packed up life in Quesnel, found homes for Anna and Max and left Canada behind. It wasn't as simple as that, of course. Initially I was assigned a guest room at Cluny. When I sought out Bettina, the Cluny Focalizer, to ask about a permanent member's room, she said that there was only one member's room available just then. A corner room, tucked down a little corridor, sharing a bathroom with one other person.

"Who?"

"Keiko." Bettina didn't look at me.

Keiko, Stewart's partner.

"It's been posted for three weeks. I don't know why it hasn't been taken," Bettina said.

I knew why. The presence of the Mystery School was palpable.

"Take a couple of days and think about it. You don't need to decide until the New Year."

I walked out of her office slowly and went up to see the room. It faced east and south, was right next to the bathroom and very quiet. It needed painting. Stewart's shoes were lined up next to Keiko's in the hall.

Later that morning I met Stewart for a cup of tea.

"Why don't you take this room next to Keiko? It's a lovely couples' space."

"I like the room I've got," he said.

I went to the Sanctuary and meditated. After a long time, I seemed to hear a voice speaking in my head. "It's great that you think you have changed enough to be here differently. Now, can you share this corner of the house with Stewart and Keiko? If not, perhaps you're not ready to come back yet."

I opened my eyes and stared out the window.

The next day I told Bettina I'd take the room.

I also needed a staff position. The only one open was Cluny Homecare. I said yes. So did Management. I was back.

It wasn't easy stepping into the Homecare position at the start. Two of the people in the department knew me slightly, the other not at all, but it took them a while to accept me. I was reminded of my Experience Weeks, of guests who looked warily at me, unsure whether or not they trusted me. I waited patiently, holding them the same way I used to hold guests, ignoring my occasional headaches. Meanwhile I felt my own love of Homecare return.

Even though the department members kept an emotional distance, I discovered that I enjoyed holding guests in Homecare even more than I did in the Guest Department. My theme on Monday mornings was transformation. Most guests learned to enjoy the department within a shift or two. I smiled when I remembered it had taken me three months.

In the aftermath of the Sex and Spirit Conference, Cluny Homecare had become a department of people in relationship. Long-term, new, straight, gay, long distance, good, bad, stable and volatile, all were represented in our group. I was the token celibate. When relationships went badly, the sharings were tearful and the work suffered. I thought hard work could balance out emotional storms. I even said so once. But when the person I was speaking to turned pained eyes on me, I remembered how little teaching had helped me after Paul's death.

"Just do what you can," I said in the end. "Take care of yourself."

Work did help me cope with Stewart and Keiko's relationship. Keiko flirted with other men, sulked, made up with Stewart – and as their next door neighbour, I couldn't avoid knowing. Sometimes her door would slam, or the sound of their angry voices would spill over into the rest of the flat. The instability was infectious. I still cared more for Stewart than anyone else. Keiko and I coped with the living arrangement because we were scrupulously polite when we had to speak and we ignored each other the rest of the time. Between the tension with her and the continuing faint uncertainty in Homecare, life was tolerable but not easy.

One afternoon I was hoovering the entrance way, worrying about the department budget and wondering what I could do, short of violence, to make people use the mat before tracking in dirt from the drive. As I dragged Kermit, the aging hoover, into the corners, a guest paused on her way into the lounge and grinned.

"You're wearing the same colour as the hoover," she said, pointing down at Kermit. "You look like a team."

I had on my favourite sweatshirt in emerald green.

"You could be an advertisement," she added.

And then I saw it. The whole department wearing tops that matched the colours of the cheerful, smiling Henry hoovers that everyone loved. We needed at least five new hoovers that we couldn't afford to replace ailing, aged ones. We needed a donation. Perhaps the Henry Vacuum Company would give us one.

I put the idea to the others at the end of the shift.

"Tell me if you think this is stupid, or if you're insulted at the idea of appearing in an advertisement for a hoover."

"It's brilliant. I want to wear red," said Lizzy, one of the LCG guests. The others nodded enthusiastically. I beamed.

The next afternoon, seven of us wearing red, green, blue or yellow tops, posed with seven matching hoovers on the green lawn in front of Cluny. Someone took photos.

We lay on the grass with the Henrys, embraced them, jumped them, straddled them and laughed ourselves into fits. The next day I composed a heart-rending letter to the head of marketing of the Henry Vacuum Company, saying how much we loved the Henrys, how hard they worked with many different people and how desperate we were for new ones.

A month later I received a letter from the president of the company, and *eight* new hoovers, two of each colour. Everyone in the department was thrilled. Cluny Homecare became the toast of the Foundation Service departments. We were a team at last, and we'd just won gold.

After that life in the department ran smoothly. Now when I felt a headache lurking, I let the others take over instead of soldiering on through the shift.

My headaches came and went irregularly. A friend, Lilli Anathal, offered some energy work on my knotted shoulders and neck. After one session she handed me a glass of water. "Is there still some lingering grief for Paul?"

"There is always some lingering grief for Paul." I frowned at the glass. "It should be finished, but it isn't. I don't think it will ever go away completely."

"You could write about it."

"Good God, no. I don't want to go there again. Aside from the headaches, life is finally going well; I don't need to turn over rocks from the past, thanks."

"I think it might help with the headaches."

Silence.

"Of course, if you prefer the headaches ..."

I glared at her. She smiled.

I hadn't had therapy since I'd left the Foundation in 2000. I hadn't felt the need of it in Canada while I was writing my novel. Even though it was fiction, I'd written about my own issues, used the writing to be a kind of therapist to myself. Maybe Lilli Anathal had a point. I'd mostly stopped writing since returning to the Foundation because the days were too busy. But a week later I opened my laptop and stared at the blank screen.

Paul. I had brought no pictures of him this time either. But just sitting alone, saying his name aloud, brought back a flood of memories. Slowly my fingers began to move across the keys. *His eyes were gray blue, and the fair straight hair that flopped down over his forehead held every colour from tawny brown through deep gold, platinum and ash grey. When he touched me ....* I closed my eyes, felt that touch and tears in the back of my throat.

The days were full, but I would grab a few hours to write on weekends, and I wrote every day on a one-week retreat on Iona. I began to feel the same kind of pressure to write that I'd experienced when I was crossing Canada. Over the months the narrative extended from the early days of my relationship with Paul through our love affair and marriage. While I was at the computer I would disappear completely into that other world. It was like writing my novel, only the people were real and I couldn't change the ending. As I wrote about my previous life in Canada, I felt more and more at home in the Foundation.

That's when I became a spiritual person. When Paul was dying. This isn't just about my relationship with Paul. This is about my connection with Spirit.

When the Paul in the manuscript died, I kept writing. When I could find time. My working hours were longer as head of Homecare. Life was busier as a staff member than it had been when I was a student.

Because I'd once been a member of the Guest Department, the focalizers kept asking me to come in and speak to Experience Week groups. I finally agreed to give an Inner Life Sharing, the talk that had convinced me that Foundation people were mad in my own Experience Week.

I felt nervous the first time.

"Inner life is the experience of paying attention to the inward process, not the external one. I think a lot of us accumulate relationships, possessions, outward experiences in the first half of our lives. I did. Education, friends, jobs, a house, a partner, perhaps children. I didn't have children, but I had the rest of it." Eighteen attentive faces looked at me. I hoped they weren't just being polite.

"At some point, if we are lucky, our focus changes and we look inward instead of out. For many people it is a mid-life process, but some come to it much earlier. What causes the shift? Often a loss, of an expected promotion, or a job, the end of a marriage, the death of a parent or partner or close friend. Some kind of health crisis, perhaps. Children leaving home. Something shakes us up, makes us turn inward and ask - why? Who am I really? What have I been doing with my life? What matters to me? Then comes the inward search.

"My husband's death six months after our wedding made me wonder what my life was about. I was thirty-nine, and I felt as if I couldn't go on. What had been important to me besides my marriage was my job. But when the marriage ended, the job became meaningless. That's when I eventually began to let go, pare life down to the basics. It was a survival strategy; I couldn't handle anything else anyway. I wasn't a spiritual person and it took several years to find some ground to stand on. In the process I let go of my career, some of my friendships and a lifestyle that no longer meant anything to me. After years of rejecting God, I slowly began to accept a spiritual connection. Now I see the basics as faith in Spirit, some wisdom and a capacity for love. I still find life challenging, but I know that much of it is a mystery I'm not able to understand, and I need to live with that. "

I looked around the silent group. "Now it's your turn. We'll meditate for a few minutes, and then I'll ask you to join two other people and share whatever you want about your own search. I believe you are on one, whether you've seen it that way or not, and that's how you've ended up here this week."

A few minutes after the end of the meditation, the room filled with a quiet hum as the guests listened and spoke to each other. The focalizer gave me a thumbs up. I breathed out, shakily. I felt unexpectedly happy.

CHAPTER 32

To Stay

Pain shot through my right eye like a skewer. At least the Homecare shift was over. I sank deeper into my chair. Just a few minutes with my eyes closed, and then I'd get up and go to my room. I felt a hand on my arm.

"You have been working like someone – obsessed." It was Irmgard's voice. A member of the Homecare team. I tried to open my eyes but gave up. Even though it was a dull November afternoon the light hurt.

"I know. But the house is full of ex-members for this Foundation birthday celebration and ..."

"It is often this full in summer, and you do not work like a madwoman. Why now?"

"I ... I just don't want any of these people to compare Cluny to the good old days and find it lacking, that's all. There are people here from four different decades in the Foundation history. I want them to see Cluny at its best."

"But even if they did say that, it would only mean they were remembering their past. It would have no other meaning."

I didn't answer.

"I wondered whether ..." She hesitated.

"What?"

"Whether you are trying not ... not to see yourself as an ex-member in another year." Her voice was gentle.

I squeezed my eyelids shut, but it was no use. Tears burned their way out, and my throat closed so completely I couldn't speak. I hadn't thought anything of the kind, but now that Irmgard had said it I couldn't think of anything else.

In the hours that followed I curled up in the red leather chair by the window in my room. Sitting up kept nausea at bay and helped the headache pass more quickly. This comfortable chair was my prized possession, found in the furniture storage area the day after someone had donated it to Cluny. Migraines forced me to stop everything but thinking. When I couldn't read or write, endure light or company, I sat in the chair and thought about what might have triggered the migraine.

I would have been completely happy if I hadn't known that I was still going to have to leave Britain eventually. On my return in 2001 I'd had two years remaining on my visa. By the Foundation's fortieth birthday celebration, nearly half that period had gone. The end was looming; I couldn't bear it.

However my last visa stamp had been dated April 4, and I had another year after that. There was time. Spirit might find a way to give me what I wanted so badly. The government might change the rules. Someone British might propose marriage. I sighed.

Stewart was really the only man I cared enough for to consider marrying, but he was still with Keiko. Living next door, I was a reluctant witness to all their ups and downs. I didn't envy them their stormy relationship, but I wanted him to be happy and I didn't see how he could be. Life was easiest when he was away visiting friends and family. Then I could settle down to a steady rhythm of work, connections with friends, singing lessons, Taizé and meditation. But he wasn't away often. I slid lower in the chair. Dozed.

When I woke it was morning and my headache was gone.

I tried to lighten up around the work as Irmgard had suggested and survived the frantically busy week of the Foundation's fortieth birthday.

Keiko returned to Japan for a month that year in December. Christmas in the Foundation was my favourite time of year, and her absence meant I could enjoy it fully. I loved the decorations, the fires, the absence of guests, all of which meant the members grew closer to each other. Without Keiko, Stewart was more available for sharing meals, conversations, cups of tea and beer.

The week long Angels and Mortals game was the start of the Christmas celebrations. This was a Findhorn Foundation variation on the "draw a name and give presents anonymously to the person you've drawn" game. That year I drew Margo as my mortal.

"Who is this Margo? I didn't see her name on the LCG list." LCG was the only guest program that continued over Christmas.

"Blonde, Belgian, she just did Experience Week and she's staying on as Joe's personal guest," said Derek, who was organizing the game that year.

"So I have to act like an angel to someone who is only here for sex."

Derek laughed. "Think of it as a seasonal challenge."

I groaned. Love affairs were playing havoc with the Homecare Department that month. At least two Homecare people were so distracted by fights and breakups that their work was either non-existent or done in black despair. I suppose I envied Margo; I was tired of being the Homecare Celibate. Life in general was wonderful, but I missed the warmth of sexual intimacy, the kind of grounded, loving connection I'd once had with Paul, that I wished I could have with Stewart. But I reminded myself that Christmas was the season of peace and goodwill and tried harder.

One morning in January, as I was folding kitchen laundry while sheets and pillowcases whirled around in the washing machines and towels in the dryers, Bettina came into the laundry.

"Hi. What's up?"

"We're looking for someone to focalize the new member program here in Cluny, and no one's applied," she said.

"Oh." The one-year student program was changing; it would now be a three-month program followed by a six-month period for people who wanted to stay on as members. I'd opposed the changes. I put the folded kitchen laundry into a basket, pulled towels out of the dryers onto the table and then began to heave clean wet sheets out of Romulus, the bigger washing machine, into another laundry basket.

"I think you'd be good."

I hauled the laundry basket over to the dryer and straightened up. "I wouldn't be good, Bettina. I didn't support the program change in the first place. Besides, I like the job I have."

"You'd be setting up the program along with the Park person. It would be a halftime job; you'd still be able to work in Homecare."

"But not focalize it."

"No. But Irmgard is ready to focalize, isn't she?" Irmgard had been in Homecare nine months. She was more than ready; she was getting restless. I changed direction.

"My visa only has a year and a bit left. I wouldn't be able to finish the second group before I had to leave."

"I know."

"And you still want me to apply?"

She nodded. I pushed the last of the wet sheets into Desert Storm, the big, industrial dryer, and started the drying cycle. The noise almost drowned out Bettina's parting comment.

"You'd be good if you wanted to be. Think about it."

I did think about it, and the more I thought the less I liked the idea. I had so little time left, a year and three or four months at most. I didn't want to spend them setting up a program when I wouldn't even be around to make sure it succeeded. I was happy in Homecare. The Red-Suited Woman part of me kicked angrily.

But there it was. I'd learned to love facilitating Homecare. Now I had to learn to let go. And Irmgard *was* ready for a staff position. She would be an excellent Homecare focaliser but if there were no job opening here, she would go elsewhere. I remembered my New Year's Resolution to be more attuned to Spirit and snarled.

That night I dreamed of Paul. He was packing a bag for a sailing trip to Hawaii.

"You'll be gone so long," I said tearfully. He smiled at me, but he didn't speak. I reached out my arms to him as the dream ended.

When I woke I remembered how fully he had lived, as long as he could. He'd never slowed down, coasted or taken the easy route. Lived until .... I tensed in the darkness of my bedroom. Leaving the Foundation was a kind of death. My life here had a termination date, even if I didn't know exactly when it was. My eyes burned. I felt tears running down the back of my throat.

I thought about Paul as I lay awake. Thought about how much I had admired his courage and his determination, his commitment to living.

Two days later I said yes to the new job and negotiated three weeks off before it began. I had decided not to return to Canada for my holiday this year. Instead I would visit my cousins on the west coast of Scotland, explore the Isle of Skye, and finish with a retreat week at Traigh Bhan, the Foundation house on Iona. I'd leave for the coast in mid-May.

I had waited as late as possible to send my passport to the Home Office for my final, one-year visa extension, trusting that the longer I delayed within the time frame of my last stamp, the more time I would buy myself. It was dinner time on a Friday night, a week before my holiday, when the passport came back. I was toasting Irmgard as the new focalizer of the Homecare Department when the bus driver from the Park handed me the envelope. I ripped it open and flipped through the pages of my passport looking for the new stamp with the exit date. Found it. February 28, 2004. The anniversary of the date I had entered Great Britain to begin FYP in 1997.

I stared at it blankly. I'd been expecting a date at least two months later, with luck, three. But this... *February!* Not late spring or early summer. Not a year from now. February. The 28th. They hadn't even given me the Leap Year day. A tidal wave of rage surged straight up into my throat. I stood up, knocking over my glass of wine, and fled from the dining room. Upstairs I slammed the door of my room so hard the windows rattled.

"You *bastard*! I've been spiritual. I've done my work. I've met every fucking test you've given me. Why do you keep raising the bar? Why can't I have a couple of months more? *Why can't I get what I want for once?*"

I flung pillows against the wall, kicked the furniture, pounded my hands and flailed my feet. Then I cried. When I finally stopped, exhausted, the silence was absolute. The date still read February 28, 2004. Less than ten months away.

CHAPTER 33

Ways and Means

My internal temper tantrum wore itself out eventually. I was still angry, but I decided to put the whole leaving issue aside until I went on holiday. I would think about it then. I was packing for the west coast of Scotland, when Lilli Anathal knocked on my door. She glanced at my suitcase, lying half-filled on the bed.

"I have news, a gift to take away with you." She smiled. "Keiko tells me she and Stewart have broken up. She is with someone else. I tell you so you can think what this means while you are away. Maybe it makes a difference."

I sat down. Despite all their quarrels, Keiko and Stewart had been together so long that this news was a shock. I couldn't take it in. Hope flared up so sharply that I didn't realize I was frightened. What I had wanted for three years had finally happened. Would it make a difference? I put a sweater into the suitcase with trembling hands.

"Thanks. Thanks for telling me."

I had trouble falling asleep that night.

Driving away from Cluny in a rental car the next day I felt hope and joy bubbling up inside me. By the time I reached the west coast it had fizzled out. Stewart hadn't cared enough for me to resist Keiko three years ago. What had changed?

I spent ten days on the west coast, first with my relatives, then on Skye. The weather was cool and sunny with occasional rain showers that created rainbows but never lingered. My elderly cousins were quiet and peaceful as always, connecting me with family energy.

On Skye I saw mountains tall and dreary in cloud and fog, radiant in sunlight. I sometimes stopped the car to stare at the views, transfixed by the whirling changes of colour in the sea as clouds scudded across the sky. I watched the ewes with their new-born lambs beside quiet lochs and gazed out at distant islands. I imagined Celts, Vikings and warring clansmen sailing and rowing their boats in and out of the bays all along the coast and among the islands. When I discovered that the car had a CD player I bought some CDs, laments sung in Gaelic. I felt as if I had taken root in the land and the culture. I never wanted to leave.

After five days in Skye I returned the rental car and took the bus to Iona. If nothing changed this was going to be my last week at Traigh Bhan. As a Foundation member. Technically I could come back as a guest, but I refused to think about myself as a visitor in a place I considered home. I slept in the upstairs bedroom, glorying in the views to the north, east and west. The light and sea changed constantly. The island of Mull appeared and disappeared in the mist with rainbows arching over it as rain alternated with sunshine. I watched the shaggy, red-haired Highland calves nuzzle their mothers and struggled to come to terms with leaving. I did not want to feel like a helpless victim again so I wrestled with the issue in prayer and meditation. It was hard to ask because I was so afraid of being rejected.

I don't want to leave. I love living here, I work hard, I contribute a lot, I have a place here and there is nothing for me in Canada. Canada is where I was widowed and nearly destroyed, first by grief, then by Marilyn the Madwoman, and finally by loneliness. I don't want to return. Please, may there be a way to stay here.

I sat with that for the week but I could feel no response, not in my dreams, my mind or my meditations. Spirit persistently remained the old white man God of my childhood. But I remembered with gritted teeth that I was now much more spiritually mature. In the end I prayed for the best and the highest for my future, whatever that was. With a clear postscript: *You know what I want. Could You just give it to me?* A voice like a six-year-old. But

I couldn't shut it off.

The day I returned to the Foundation, I decided that Spirit might choose to be silent, but I was going to help myself.

There was only one way to stay: marry someone British. What kind of person married in order to secure a visa? I shrank from the word prostitute. After Paul's death I had promised myself I would not take second best, even if it meant I never married again. But leaving .... I stared out the window.

I pictured Stewart, his rumpled hair, brown eyes and strong, stocky body. His grin. My affection for him hadn't changed since I'd first talked to him at Christmas in 1997, despite his ex-wife in Glasgow, his three-year connection with Keiko and the disruption of our friendship. But would he consider marriage? He had suggested an affair five years ago, but he'd never reopened the subject.

It's not selling myself if I love him, I thought. I do. He makes me laugh, we've been best friends ever since we met except for Keiko, and I've always wanted to go to bed with him. Now that ... if his relationship with her is really over ... It doesn't feel second best. Just ... different. But I felt nervous even thinking about it.

The new job began. I stayed halftime in Homecare and met regularly with my work partner in the Park to map out what the Living Education Staff Program would look like. Irmgard focalized Homecare so beautifully that I saw that my decision to step down had been the right one.

Time seemed to creep and to race, simultaneously. One Thursday night, when there were only eight months left, I asked Stewart to come out for beer with me. He beamed.

"Aye, I'd like that. I need to get in some practice at dominoes too, before the next season starts. Too long a gap over the summer. Are you willing?"

Stewart had played dominoes with a local pub team for a couple of years. I thought dominoes was a nothing sort of game, just an excuse to drink beer, but when he beat me nine games out of ten that first night I conceded there might be some level of skill to it.

He grinned and said he would teach me.

That first evening led to a weekly beer and dominoes date on Thursdays that became the highlight of my week. We settled on a pub in the east end of Forres and walked to it through the Cluny Woods. Virtually every Thursday night that summer was clear, and we saw glowing sunsets and exquisite glimpses of Findhorn Bay and Findhorn Village from the hill. We laughed a lot, even more when I began to win and we had to use beer mats to keep track of the score. Some nights we wandered back hand in hand in moonlight filtered through the trees. But the dates remained pleasant platonic evenings, and I was afraid to raise the question of marriage.

Time was running. One night in August I gathered my courage. We were sitting at an end table, close to the fire and far enough away from anyone else for privacy. He'd finished his first beer while I still nursed my half-pint, and we had not yet brought out the dominoes board. I gripped my hands together and tried not to wring them.

"Stewart, you've been my best friend for years, ever since our first Christmas in Cluny." I took a nervous swig of beer and seized my hands again to keep from draining the glass. Stewart looked mildly interested.

"I want to ask you … whether you'd consider … well, I want to stay in the Foundation. The only way is marriage … and … you're the only man I can ask. I care about you. Would you think about marrying me?"

Stewart was silent. Around us local people drank beer, laughed and talked.

"Don't feel you have to answer immediately," I said. "Think about it. If you say yes I'll know it's because you're willing to do me a favour, not because you're in love with me, but take whatever time you need. It's a big thing I'm asking you."

He'd been staring down into his empty glass, but now he looked up with kind, steady brown eyes.

"I've been considering it for some time already," he said. I nearly burst into tears of gratitude. "But there are two problems. One is I'm actually not divorced yet, although the papers should come soon." My heart stopped. I'd had no idea. "The second is ... I ... it wouldn't be a sexual relationship. I don't feel that way about you now. So you think about that. Would you be content?"

I stared at him, feeling as if I'd just stepped off solid ground into nothingness. *It wouldn't be a sexual relationship?* I thought every man was interested in sex. *Wait. Don't panic and don't speak. Feel into it.* As I sat there, mute, Stewart went off to get two more beers. I looked into the fire. When he came back with another pint for him and a half for me, I took a long drink and forced a smile.

"Let's both think about it and talk again in two weeks. After Laura's wedding? Will I get the board and the doms?" He nodded. I don't remember who won at dominoes that night. We walked home through the woods hand in hand, in silence.

There were three weddings planned at Cluny for the end of the summer. Laura's was the first. She'd had a long association with the Foundation but lived in Forres. The other two were couples in the house, Patrick and Georgete and Derek and Monika. The Taizé singers had been rehearsing for the past three weeks.

I was grateful that I felt delighted, and not jealous, about the wedding plans all around me. Homecare cleaned all of the massive windows on the three sides of the ballroom, inside and out. The ballroom was the setting for Laura and Ian's reception, for the dancing for Patrick's and Georgete's wedding and for the actual ceremony for Derek and Monika.

Only six months left before my visa expired. Laura's Italian family was coming over for the wedding. One afternoon she found me at break and asked me to step outside. We took our tea down into the garden and sat on a bench in the sunshine. I could hear the water falling into the pond behind us.

"You know Ian is widowed," she said. I nodded. "Well some of his former in-laws don't really want to come to our wedding. They disapprove of remarriage." She stared into the apple trees, where small green apples dotted the boughs. "I could ignore it, I suppose, but it feels really important for his son to maintain contact with them. I'd like to have a short ritual of forgiveness in the service, to help people let go of the past. What do you think?"

"It's a beautiful idea," I said. "So beautiful that I'm surprised I haven't seen it before. Lots of people must feel ambivalent at weddings for a whole bunch of reasons. I know I have."

She nodded. "So have I. Will you hold it?"

It shouldn't have been a surprise, but it was. The garden became a green and gold blur. I passed my hand over my eyes and blinked. "Yes, of course. I'd be honoured. I hope I can do it justice." She hugged me.

Because I was going to have an active part in all three weddings I decided to buy a wedding 'frock' and hat. Normally I wore only casual clothes from charity shops. This would be different.

By the day of Laura's wedding I had a black, silk chiffon dress with a V-neck, cap sleeves and a trail of flowers embroidered erratically down the front in a way that miraculously emphasized both curves and slimness. A handkerchief hemline dipped and drifted, making my legs look better than they had in years. I wore new shoes and a pale pink pashmina shawl that matched the embroidery on the dress. The hat was a broad-brimmed black straw, with a large bow and tiny black feathers rising above the crown. It was such a wonderfully feminine outfit that I was unnerved putting it on. I hadn't looked this feminine since – since my own wedding day, fourteen years ago.

My wedding pictures were locked in storage in Canada, but I could see that young woman, radiant with love and happiness, glowing with confidence in the future. I felt my lips tremble. I would never be that confident again, now that I knew how quickly happiness could vanish. The glamourous woman in the mirror looked at me with sad, frightened eyes. What difference did a hat and dress really make? With or without them, I was a vulnerable, celibate, middle-aged woman.

Then I straightened up. *You look terrific. Anyway this day is about Laura and Ian.* I put on lipstick and left my room, pulling the hat brim low over my face.

I found it hard to look directly at anyone on my way to the

sanctuary, but peoples' jaws dropped when they saw me and I blushed under the open admiration.

The sanctuary was so full of people that the Taizé singers, including me, had to stand at the back. The brim of my hat kept hitting the wall so I took it off and shoved it underneath the chair in front. We sang Laura and Ian into the sanctuary. Light from the north window brightened the tall plants that framed them. The celebrant welcomed everyone, her greeting echoed by the Italian translator. Then she gave me my cue and I walked up to stand beside her.

Even though Laura's idea of a forgiveness plea was brilliant, even though she had given me lots of warning, I choked up before I completed the first sentence.

"Marriage is a huge commitment, not easy to make and every couple needs the full support of their friends and family. I - believe all of us who are wedding guests want to be able to offer this. But often we carry difficult personal memories of past betrayals, failures and - and losses with us to weddings, memories that haunt and distract us through the ceremony. In order that each of us can be fully present today for Laura and Ian, I'd like us to take a couple of moments of silence, so we can acknowledge these memories, forgive others and ourselves for old heartaches, and release the past, if we need to, before bringing our full attention here."

By the time Laura's family had absorbed the Italian translation almost everyone else was in tears too. I was aware of the video camera pointing its red eye relentlessly at me and wished fervently that I was still wearing my hat.

After the ceremony a middle-aged woman spoke to me in the washroom. She wore high pink heels and a fussy, flowered dress that looked too young for her.

"I want to thank you for what you said during the service." Her eyes met mine in the mirror. "This is the first wedding I've been to since – well, since my husband left me for someone younger. I was dreading it. But now I think – I wonder if I shouldn't just forgive him and move on. Thanks for the encouragement."

"Thank you for telling me. Maybe I can forgive the man who

was videotaping me crying the whole time I spoke."

She laughed. I could see the gallantry in her elaborate dress and high-heeled shoes. She was trying hard despite her own disappointment.

Stewart joined the reception, and we drank champagne and danced together in the ballroom.

"Nice dress."

Maybe it was to his credit that he wasn't dazzled as other people had been. He saw me.

Afterwards we walked to the Ramnee in Forres for a drink. A detached part of me watched him as we talked and laughed. I cared so much about him, I wanted so badly to stay in the Foundation, but – I remembered something I had once said to Paul. *Marriage is a sacrament. A heart and mind and soul connection, not just a legal contract.* A physical, sexual connection too. Like Laura and Ian. We were best friends, Stewart and I. Was that enough?

That night in bed I clutched Bear. Paul and I had been best friends as well as lovers, and eventually we had married. Friendship was a wonderful basis for marriage.

"Not without sex," said the voice in my mind. "Marriage without sex is a sham. You couldn't make it look real, and Stewart would end up with another Keiko in record time. You'd lose everything, your best friend, your visa and your self-respect. And you swore you'd never accept second best after marriage with Paul."

I stared wet-eyed into the darkness. There was no choice. Not really.

I would leave on February 28th, 2004, in six months time.

CHAPTER 34

A Divine Invitation

Two nights after Laura's wedding, Stewart came to my room for a cup of tea. He sat in the red leather chair by the window while I slumped on the bed, my back against the wall. Behind him the sky was darkening. The days were getting noticeably shorter, and the stars had reappeared at night.

"I've been thinking about marriage since Laura and Ian's ceremony." I stared into my tea. "They have a real marriage on all levels. It made me realize that I … well, I don't think I can marry without passion as well as a loving friendship. I … I need to withdraw my offer of marriage." I couldn't stop the tears but I managed to look at him. He got up from the chair, sat down on the bed, set his tea carefully on the floor and put his arms around me.

"Aye. I know."

"I guess I have to leave." My shoulders shook. He pulled me down beside him on the bed. We lay like that for a long time as I wept. Our tea grew cold. The moon rose and shone in the east window.

"Would you like me to stay the night?"

I nodded. A while later I peeled off my jeans and slid under the covers in a T-shirt. He wore his underwear. I fell asleep quickly.

Sometime in the night I woke. Stewart had curled around me, his groin pressed against my backside. His underwear had disappeared, and he was very much awake.

"Hey," I muttered, as he stroked my thighs. "What are you doing? I thought you said you weren't interested in sex with me."

"I did say that, but I was wrong." He pulled me around to face him. "Could we discuss it later and just focus on this now, do you think?"

I was still laughing when he kissed me.

When my alarm rang in the morning, I woke happy. Stewart blinked and looked about him as if puzzled, saw me, hesitated and smiled.

"I'll be off then." He rubbed an unshaven cheek against mine, flung on his clothes and bolted from the room. My happiness wilted. I got out of bed slowly and stared out at the sun rising over the trees. For a few minutes in the night I'd hoped ... But this was only a one night stand that made no difference.

Stewart avoided my eyes at breakfast, as if he was afraid I'd expect an engagement ring.

I knew I had to leave the Foundation, but when I sat in a Council meeting later that week with twenty-three other people who didn't need permission to stay, I couldn't bring myself to speak.

"I never have time for my art," said one woman. "I'm thinking of leaving Foundation membership and taking a room in the village just so I have more scope for creativity." I wanted to scream at her to shut up, but I was afraid to open my mouth in case I couldn't stop. I couldn't focus on the business agenda. Afterwards I nearly crawled back to my room.

I felt too old to start over again in Canada. Just thinking about it exhausted me. With or without spare time, I loved life in the Foundation. All I wanted to do was to stay, work and serve. I had committed to the Foundation as deeply as I had to my marriage. And it was all ending the same way, through an act of Spirit. I wanted to curse God all over again.

Ironically I had agreed to do an Inner Life Sharing for the Experience Week that was about to start.

On Sunday night I walked slowly into the Beechtree Room. I looked around the circle, while the focalizer introduced me and the guests smiled politely. They might be at the start of a long-term stay. I had to leave. A wave of envy broke over me, and I couldn't speak for a few minutes. The room remained quiet. No one seemed bothered by my silence. I imagined them thinking this was how it was done here.

Finally I found my voice. I could hear the quaver as I spoke.

"I've done a lot of Inner Life Sharings in the past year and enjoyed them. But tonight ... tonight is the first time I'm going to speak about my connection with Spirit knowing that I ... I'm required to do something I have huge resistance to. I have to leave the Foundation in February; my visa is up, and it's breaking my heart."

A guest across the circle raised her eyes and stared directly at me. Her shoulders tensed. The quality of the silence in the room changed too. Why should they have to cope with my grief? I wished I'd cancelled.

"Tonight I'll say what I usually say but ... a part of me feels like a fraud. Like I'm the last person who should be doing this sharing if I ... I can't live up to my own words. I need to acknowledge that first. I am trying-" my voice cracked. I took a deep breath. "I am trying to follow what I believe but it doesn't get easier after five years here. It gets harder. I once thought transformation happened quickly and perhaps it does for some. But for me it's obviously a lifetime process."

I looked around again, and began. It was the hardest Inner Life sharing I had ever done. None of the guests spoke to me when I finished an hour later. But the focalizer hugged me.

"It was perfect. From the heart. It doesn't get any better. Thank you from me and from them."

There had never been a more beautiful autumn in my years in the Foundation. Rain came only fitfully, and the sun shone for days at a time. The gardens were brilliant with colour. A week before her wedding, Georgete asked me if I would read a poem by Hafiz, a fourteenth-century Sufi poet, during the service.

"And you'll sit with Stewart at the head table, yes?"

"Sure, I'd love to."

She handed me a book of Hafiz's poems, *I Heard God Laughing.* A day later, I flipped through the book. I'd never read Hafiz before. One of the poems stopped me dead.

A Divine Invitation

You have been invited to meet
The Friend.

No one can resist a Divine Invitation.
That narrows down all our choices
To just two:
We can come to God
Dressed for dancing
Or
Be carried on a stretcher
To God's ward.

I gaped at it. My voice shook as I read it aloud. "Dressed for dancing." With a start, I remembered my Life Purpose eight years before, to celebrate God through dance. I closed my eyes for a moment, then raised my head, stretched and looked about. My room felt too small.

I took the poetry book and left the building. At the back of the property a high brick wall separates the Peace Garden from the woods. I sat down there on a bench. Sunlight filtered through the trees. The only flowers in the garden were white, shining like beacons in a sea of green. I read the poem again.

"Be carried on a stretcher to God's ward." How familiar. No matter how hard I tried to "do it right," to please, to be perfect, it changed nothing. Other people didn't try to be perfect, and their lives worked out. A part of me remained detached as a slow heat began to burn inside me. At my most aligned, I'd had my greatest loss; Paul had died. Fourteen years ago.

"I'll be all right," I'd told him. My great heroic moment. But that had only lasted while he lived. Once he'd died I hadn't been heroic, and I hadn't ever been all right. I had wanted to die too, but despite minor ailments, I'd remained relentlessly healthy, doomed to live. I had decided not to commit suicide literally, but – the truth was - I'd tried to kill off the best part of myself, the loving, compassionate woman. I'd forsaken my family, my friends and my job to mourn Paul. I'd retreated, shut down the heart that had opened with him.

All this time I had told myself it was grief, but underneath the grief I now knew was rage. All those odd moments, when I was suddenly so furious without much cause, they must have originated from this rage at God.

Like my rage at Marilyn ...

Needy, pathetic Marilyn, acting out in the way my family found intolerable, just as I was doing. While I was denying my own rage and thinking myself a hero for loving Paul so much, there she was, a mirror, "loving" me and reflecting my own distortion. What had she said to the minister? "I don't care if I'm dead, if I'm with her."

No wonder I'd wanted to kill her.

I closed my eyes. The Peace Garden was silent.

Had I ever come to God "dressed for dancing?" On the morning of my wedding, perhaps. And when Paul was dying, I had been fully committed and fully loving, the right words had come and he had been released. I could love Paul that well, but not myself. Not life. Not Spirit. My attempts to come closer to Spirit here in the Foundation had not confronted the depths. Not until now.

A long time passed while I sat with this new slant on the last fourteen years of my life.

What now?

Perhaps coming to God "dressed for dancing" meant being willing to move in tune with the music and the will of Spirit. I flexed my feet in my sandals and looked down at them. The skin looked almost green in that light, as if I were under water. My face was wet.

I glanced back at the poem. "No one can resist/ A Divine

Invitation." I could weep and look backwards forever, but it changed nothing. I was still going to be carried in the direction of God's Ward.

I had five and a half months left in the Foundation. I thought of Paul, living as fully as he could, loving me right to the end. Loss. Acceptance. I drew a long, shaking breath. If acceptance was dancing, I would try to dance out my five remaining months with love and trust that beyond my departure, there would be something more.

Georgete and Patrick's wedding was a huge Foundation event. Almost everyone was there, including ex-members. Cluny Sanctuary was too small to hold the crowd so the ceremony took place in the garden. The Taizé Choir sang as Patrick came down the path in a kilt, accompanied by Stewart and a group of Foundation men. Then Georgete arrived, led by Cluny women. When the bride and groom looked into each other's faces, Patrick's eyes overflowed. My throat closed. They looked so much in love. I thought of my own wedding day. This time I kept my hat on while I read the poem Georgete had chosen, and my face stayed in shadow.

Later in the beautifully decorated dining room, Stewart smiled at me as I sat down beside him. I smiled back. We weren't meant to marry, and he had recognized it. But he was still the man who listened to me, shared his beer, made me laugh, hugged me when I needed a hug. Still my best friend.

Two weeks after Patrick and Georgete, Derek from Aberdeen married Monika from Germany in the ballroom on a Sunday morning. Monika was eight months pregnant and barefoot because her feet were too swollen for her shoes. She wore white silk with a wreath of roses on her long, rippling auburn hair and looked like a fertility goddess. Derek was radiant with happiness.

Stewart and I had commissioned a photographer to take their wedding pictures as a joint wedding gift. After she finished with the bridal couple, she took a picture of us together under one of the apple trees. We look marvellous in the photo, Stewart in his kilt and me in my wedding guest finery, apples reddening on the bough behind us. My silk chiffon skirt drifts in the breeze, and Stewart's eyes turn toward me as if he were intent on pursuit.

One regret I had was that I'd nearly always gone to Canada for my holidays. So I asked Stewart to show me Glasgow, his home city. He was leaving the day after the wedding for a six-week compassionate leave in the south of England to take care of his mother, who had been in a car accident. We agreed to meet in Glasgow when he came north.

Monika gave birth to her child in Cluny at the end of October. As part of her support team I was there. I'd never been present at a birth. Toward the end she struggled on hands and knees, her hair, half-braided, hanging in tangled disarray over one shoulder, sweat glistening on her distended body, breathing out in great laboured groans through the contractions. I watched helplessly as her body tightened and relaxed, turned livid with the strain of the next contraction while she cried out wordlessly in pain. When the baby's head finally emerged, one midwife reached to receive it and then said, "The cord is around the neck. Stop pushing, Monika." I felt my heart constrict. Monika froze. The second midwife reached for the scissors and clamp, cut the cord and talked Monika through two more rapid contractions until the baby slid grey-blue into waiting hands. A boy. The midwife took him over to the oxygen and encouraged him to breathe. My heart started again with a thump. After a few agonizing moments his colour slowly changed to pink, and he began to make a soft chirping noise. Derek crossed the room to cradle the baby and take him to Monika.

"My son," she whispered. I watched the three of them curled together on the bed, the archetypal man, woman and child. Birth, death, rebirth. Faith.

I lived in the sunshine of those days, as time simultaneously slowed down and slid away from me.

In mid-November I slipped away out of the Foundation to meet Stewart as he returned from his leave. We hadn't spent a second night together until now. It felt like an assignation.

I took the train down to Glasgow and a taxi to the hotel Stewart had chosen. When I entered the room he emerged from the shower, wrapped in a towel, and gave me a damp hug.

I tugged at the towel, which came off. "It's great to see you. How is your mother?"

"Later."

We spent four days touring the city and four nights making love. Once I would have held back, guarding my heart. Now I was determined to live every day fully. The November weather was frosty, but nothing could chill Stewart's love for Glasgow. He made it beautiful in my eyes. We walked, visited famous churches and historical sites, saw his secondary school and his art college, checked out bookstores, an art gallery, parks, wandered along the Clyde River, and he told me the history of the city.

We had a seafood dinner on the third night in a posh art deco restaurant. Stewart had once run a seafood restaurant himself on the Isle of Man.

"I can't eat lobster. The year my wife was pregnant she wanted lobster all the time. Whenever my back was turned she'd have another one out of the freezer. She ate all the profit I made and when the baby was born on New Year's Eve, I couldn't afford to go to the hospital; I had to work all night."

I ate sliced smoked salmon with lime and pink peppercorns as an appetizer while Stewart had mussels. We had a glass of house white wine each, intending to be conservative, and it was so delicious we ordered a bottle. I had pan-seared scallops with celeriac in a champagne and orange butter sauce, and Stewart ordered roast halibut with fried oysters. He topped off dinner and dessert with a glass of port. I simply sat and digested. It was the best meal out that I'd had in my years in Scotland.

We hadn't mentioned February once in the course of the days in Glasgow. But lying in his arms after our lovemaking later that night I looked at him. I could just make out his profile in the light from the street lamp.

"The last time I left the Foundation it was hard, but I knew I could come back. This time is much harder. I can't do more than visit, ever again. Will you promise me something? I want ... it would help ... could you stay present as the date draws closer and not wander off and get involved with someone because she's going to be around when I am gone?"

He tightened his arms and kissed my hair. "Aye. I will."

I remember the month Paul was dying in the hospital as one of the most beautiful and vital periods of our relationship, when only love mattered. My last months in the Foundation were like that, luminous with passion, love, and celebration. I lived in the present, as Paul had, knowing that these days were brighter and more precious because the future was shadowed.

The days dwindled. I was tuned out of my LESP position of supervising new staff, out of the Cluny Focus group and finally out of Homecare. I began to pack. The spring cleaning of my room, the last work I would do for Cluny, became a ceremony.

Stewart and I were sharing his bed every night. All the flowers I received from my different groups went into vases in his room until it looked like a funeral parlour. Every time I went in, I smiled and cried simultaneously.

He came to my final Taizé evening and my farewell meditation and sat opposite me at the leaving dinner on the Friday night. For once he didn't cook so we could eat together at the huge family table. His face crumpled, just for a moment, when the person beside him said something about my departure. I caught my breath in surprise. I'd been so focused on my own feelings that I hadn't thought about his.

That was my last dinner in Cluny dining room. On Saturday Stewart took me out to dinner to a restaurant in Nairn where we'd celebrated his fiftieth birthday the year before. Sunday we ate Chinese takeout in his room. We didn't make love the last two nights, just lay together silently, holding hands. I listened to his deep breathing and felt the warmth from his body and wondered if I'd ever have another lover.

My back was straight and my eyes dry as I walked through Heathrow Airport with a one-way ticket, two hours before midnight on February 28th, 2004. I waited for the airport officials to notice that I'd spent nearly six years there, but no one even looked at my visa stamp. To them I was just another tourist.

As I sat in the Departure Lounge, I watched a dark-haired little girl, about three years old, play with her stuffed monkey. She held it lovingly under her chin, half-crooning, half-singing to it, paying no attention to the chaos around her. I smiled. She looked up into my face, and held out her toy for me to see.

"What a beautiful monkey," I said. She said something I didn't catch. Then her mother called her for the pre-boarding, and she turned away.

I recalled the prayer I said the first time I flew, before my mother died, before I met Paul, before I became so angry with God. *Into thy hands I commit my spirit.*

Then I joined the lineup. *Time to dance.*

Acknowledgements

This book has been so many years in the making that many people have offered endless hours of reading and editing time.

Betsy Warland helped me add and subtract material in the Vancouver Manuscript Intensive program as well as giving me a green light when the manuscript was ready. Her colleague, Betsy Nuse, was the copy editor, steering me gracefully through the intricacies of comma usage, and out of American and British spelling into Canadian.

My wonderful Writer's Studio group from Simon Fraser University under the guidance of Wayde Compton, read and advised: Eufemia Fantetti, Jan Redford, Ayelet Tsbari, Sue Anne Linde, Jen Caldwell, and Naz Hazar. Clarissa Green, Morgan Chojnacki and Sally Halliday, Wayde Compton, Joan Flood and Julie Bitek continued the process.

Michael Julian Berz took the cover photograph and gave me a new image of myself in the photograph he took of me.

My Story Sisters group and Marlene Schiwy from her Autobiography workshops at UBC offered loving encouragement: Susie Brown, Susila Bryant, Myrna McTaggert and Catriona Moore.

David Spangler offered huge encouragement and an endorsement at a critical moment.

My family here in Vancouver offered reading time and loving support. Jane Sutherland, Kate Sutherland and Evan Renaerts. Kate also introduced me to the Findhorn Foundation and coached me through the labyrinth of publishing.

"A Divine Invitation" is reprinted from the Penguin publication, *I Heard God Laughing, Renderings of Hafiz,* copyright 1996 & 2006 Daniel Ladinsky and used with his permission.

If it takes a village to raise a child, it takes almost as many to inspire and create a book. I am deeply grateful.

About the Author

Leslie Hill grew up in Ontario, in Orillia and Toronto. She was a high school English teacher and a teacher-librarian in Toronto for twenty-five years before moving to the Findhorn Foundation from 1997 to 2000 and from the end of 2001 to the spring of 2004. She now lives in Vancouver, British Columbia, Canada with her cat. As a west coast woman she now gardens, practises yoga and makes granola, as well as singing in the Unitarian Church Choir, writing and playing bridge. *Dressed for Dancing* is her first book. Visit her website at www.lesliehill.ca

ALSO FROM INCITE PRESS

Make Light Work
10 Tools for Inner Knowing
by Kate Sutherland

This gem of a book introduces ten tools to help you clarify priorities, make decisions, deal with the person who drives you crazy, and prepare for challenges and opportunities.

Each of us has an exquisite inner guidance system, available 24/7. Most of us have never read the instructions. This pocket guide introduces practical tools you can use on a daily basis – at home and at work – to jumpstart your inner knowing.

Perfect for leaders, managers, entrepreneurs, consultants, parents, and anyone else who wants more grace, ease, and joy.

Available by request at your local book store, or online (including at www.makelightwork.org). Sample chapters at www.makelightwork.org.

Make Light Work in Groups
10 Tools to Transform Meetings, Companies and Communities
by Kate Sutherland

This book introduces ten tools to revolutionize how we work together – in teams, organizations, companies, and communities.

If groups are how you get (or don't get) things done, you will find an abundance of insight, inspiration and practical suggestions here. The tools will help you to increase trust, unleash collective wisdom, and nurture the joyous ease of "many hands making light work."

Each of the ten tools brings a unique perspective. Together they are a comprehensive kit, allowing you to create better outcomes in all types of group situations.

Make Light Work in Groups is a handy pocket guide for leaders, managers, entrepreneurs, activists, consultants, teachers, parents – and anyone else who wants to help groups thrive.

Both books available by request at your local book store, or online (including at www.makelightwork.org). Sample chapters at www.makelightwork.org.

CPSIA information can be obtained at www.ICGtesting.com
Printed in the USA
LVOW130120081112

306332LV00003B/1/P